RAND CORPORATION

T0303223

Developing a Skilled Workforce for the Oil and Natural Gas Industry

An Analysis of Employers and Colleges in Ohio, Pennsylvania, and West Virginia

Robert Bozick, Gabriella C. Gonzalez, Cordaye Ogletree, Diana Gehlhaus Carew

For more information on this publication, visit www.rand.org/t/RR2199

Library of Congress Cataloging-in-Publication Data is available for this publication.
ISBN: 978-0-8330-9947-1

Published by the RAND Corporation, Santa Monica, Calif.

Cover image courtesy of iStock.

Preface

The challenge of connecting employers and educators to collaboratively plan for training future workers is an enduring one—particularly for jobs that are rapidly changing because of technological advancements. This report addresses this challenge as it pertains to employers and educators in the oil and natural gas industry located in and around the Utica and Marcellus shales. The combination of horizontal drilling and hydraulic fracturing to tap natural gas has resulted in the Utica and Marcellus shales becoming major sources of natural gas supply within the United States and are predicted to bring significant long-term economic benefits to the tristate region of Ohio, Pennsylvania, and West Virginia. To inform policy decisions on how best to expand and sustain the pool of workers with knowledge and skills needed by oil and natural gas employers in the tristate region, this report summarizes the findings from surveys administered to the region's oil and gas employers and education providers.

This study has three research aims: (1) Document the knowledge and skills required by employers in the oil and natural gas industry, (2) assess the extent to which colleges are positioned to provide employers in the oil and natural gas industry with workers who have appropriate knowledge and skills for high-priority occupations, and (3) identify collaborative strategies and practices in place that connect employers in the oil and natural gas industry with educators.

This report should be of interest to oil and gas employers, education providers, and stakeholders who are embedded in the collaborative efforts already under way in the region. This report can inform the direction of these collaborations so that they can effectively utilize the relationships and resources already in place to stand up an effective and comprehensive sector-based public-private partnership that supports an oil and gas workforce development system.

This research was undertaken joinly by within RAND Labor and Population and RAND Education. Both units at RAND have built an international reputation for conducting objective, high-quality, empirical research to support and improve policies and organizations around the world. For more information on RAND Labor and Population, visit the Labor and Population homepage at http://www.rand.org/labor. For more information on RAND Education, visit the Education homepage at at http://www.rand.org/education. This research is part of RAND Labor and Population and RAND Education's collaborative efforts to promote workforce development at home and abroad by conducting cutting-edge research that helps public- and private-sector decisionmakers understand how to keep workers productive, knowledgeable, and engaged. This research was funded by the National Science Foundation under grant 1535322. Any opinions, findings, and conclusions or recommendations expressed in this material are those of the authors and do not necessarily reflect the views of the National Science Foundation.

Contents

Preface iii
Figures ix
Summary xi
Acknowledgments xvii
Abbreviations xix

CHAPTER ONE
Introduction 1
Objectives of This Study 2
Educational Requirements for New Jobs in the Oil and Natural Gas Industry 4
The Oil and Natural Gas Industry in the Tristate Region 7
The Educational Context of the Tristate Region 10
The Need for an Efficient, Effective, and Agile Sector-Based Workforce Development System in the Tristate Region 11
Organization of This Report 15

CHAPTER TWO
Data Sources 17
The RAND SHALE Survey of Employers 17
The RAND SHALE Survey of Education and Training Institutes 21
Interviews with Purposefully Selected Employers 22
Limitations of Analyses 23

CHAPTER THREE
Jobs and Skills in Demand: What Employers Need ... 25
Occupations Deemed High Priority by Employers Typically Require a Bachelor's Degree ... 27
Nearly a Quarter of Employers Reported Their Companies Had High-Priority Occupations That Require Long-Term On-the-Job Training ... 30
More Than Half of Employers Have High-Priority Occupations That Require at Least Five Years of Previous Work Experience ... 33
Employers Seek Workers with Cross-Cutting Knowledge Areas and Skills ... 35
Employers Look to On-the-Job Training to Meet Their Skills Needs ... 42
Discussion ... 43

CHAPTER FOUR
Supplying Credentials, Courses, and Training Opportunities: What Colleges Provide ... 47
Colleges in the Region Do Not Explicitly Incorporate Cross-Cutting Employability Skills in Their Programming ... 48
Most Colleges Report Supporting Students Getting Jobs in Specific Occupations Within the Oil and Natural Gas Industry but Few Have Stackable Credential Programs ... 52
Fewer Than Half the Courses Aimed at Future Workers in the Oil and Natural Gas Industry Use Contextualized Instruction ... 54
Discussion ... 55

CHAPTER FIVE
Collaborating to Build a Better Workforce ... 59
The Majority of Employers Do Not Communicate Results of Workforce Planning with Colleges ... 59
Few Employers Provide Deep or Continual Instructional, Curricular, or Material Support to Colleges ... 61
Both Colleges and Employers Point to Unwillingness as the Source for Lack of Partnerships or Collaboration ... 65
Discussion ... 68

CHAPTER SIX
Conclusion and Recommendations 71
Summary of Findings 71
Limitations 72
Recommendations 74

APPENDIX
Employer Interview Protocol 77

References 81

Figures

1.1. Postsecondary Educational Requirements of Projected Job Openings in the Oil and Natural Gas Industry from 2014 Through 2024, by Segment of the Industry 5
1.2. Map of Utica and Marcellus Shale Region 8
3.1. Percentage of Employers Reporting High-Priority Occupations 26
3.2. Percentage of Employers with High-Priority Occupations That Require Specific Levels of Education 28
3.3. Percentage of Employers with High-Priority Occupations That Require Specific Levels of On-the-Job Training Needed to Obtain Competency in High-Priority Occupations 31
3.4. Percentage of Employers with High-Priority Occupations That Require Previous Work Experience for Desired Competency 34
3.5. Percentage of Employers Reporting Types of Knowledge Needed for High-Priority Occupations 37
3.6. Percentage of Employers Reporting Specific Skills Sought for High-Priority Occupations 40
3.7. Percentage of Employers Reporting Training Provided to Employees to Meet Skills Needs in High-Priority Occupations 43
4.1. Percentage of Colleges That Offer Coursework or Instruction on Specific Knowledge That Employers Seek for High-Priority Occupations 49

4.2. Percentage of Colleges That Offer Coursework or Instruction on Specific Skills That Employers Seek for High-Priority Occupations ... 51
4.3. Percentage of Colleges That Offer Programming That Aligns with Characteristics of Sector-Based Training ... 53
4.4. Proportion of Courses Using Contextualized Instruction as Reported by Colleges ... 55
5.1. Percentage of Employers That Undertake Workforce Planning Activities with Colleges ... 60
5.2. Percentage of Employers That Provide Instructional Support to Local Colleges ... 62
5.3. Percentage of Colleges That Collaborate with Employers on Instruction ... 63
5.4. Percentage of Colleges That Collaborate with Employers on Curricula Development ... 64
5.5. Percentage of Employers that Provide Material and Financial Support to Colleges ... 65
5.6. Percentage of Employers That Report Barriers in Partnering with Colleges ... 66
5.7. Percentage of Colleges That Report Barriers in Partnering with Employers ... 67

Summary

Following a period of slow growth, natural gas production in the United States grew by more than 25 percent from 2007 to 2013 (Hausman and Kellogg, 2015). Further, the industry anticipates 1.9 million job openings through 2035 (IHS Global Inc., 2016). This unprecedented expansion has rapidly changed the employment landscape in Ohio, Pennsylvania, and West Virginia (i.e., the "tristate" region). With record growth in the industry and further demand expected, ensuring that employers have access to a prepared, skilled workforce is paramount to sustaining economic growth in the tristate region.

To inform policy discussions on how best to expand and sustain the pool of workers who have the knowledge and skills needed by oil and natural gas employers in the tristate region, this report, produced by the nonprofit, nonpartisan RAND Corporation with support from the National Science Foundation, empirically addresses three research aims:

1. We document the knowledge and skills required by employers in the oil and natural gas industry.
2. We assess the extent to which colleges are positioned to supply employers in the oil and natural gas industry with workers who have the knowledge and skills they need to succeed in the industry.
3. We identify workforce development strategies and practices to connect employers in the oil and natural gas industry with educators.

To accomplish our research aims, we analyze data from three sources: a survey of 67 oil and natural gas employers in the tristate region; in-depth interviews with a purposive sample of six oil and natural gas employers to augment survey responses; and a survey of 87 heads of postsecondary education departments that offer majors related to the oil and natural gas industry. Our analysis is anchored on "high-priority occupations" as reported by employers in the survey. *High-priority occupations* are defined as jobs that are in high demand, are critical to the company's core business, require more advanced skills (education beyond high school), and provide family-sustaining wages. All findings included in this report are based on occupations that are considered by employers to be of high priority.

Findings

- **Nearly a quarter of employers reported their companies had high-priority occupations that require *long-term* on-the-job training.** About half of employers (52 percent) reported employing high-priority occupations that require moderate-term on-the-job training (including inspectors, welders, and roustabouts) and about one in four employers (28 percent) reported having high-priority occupations that require long-term on-the-job training (including mechanics, machinists, and wellhead plumbers). Thus, for many of the oil and gas sector employers in the tristate region, it is essential to invest in and commit to providing on-the-job training to ensure their workers can adequately perform their duties.
- **More than half of employers have high-priority occupations that require at least five years of previous work experience.** Sixty-four percent reported having high-priority occupations in their companies that require at least five years of previous work experience.
- **Employers seek workers with cross-cutting knowledge areas and skills.** Employers want workers who can think critically and creatively in the context of their work, solve work-based prob-

lems, and make sound decisions at work. They also want workers who understand the fundamentals of administration and management. These *cross-cutting* knowledge areas and skills were more often reported as in demand by employers than *occupation-specific* ones.

- **Though employers desire basic cross-cutting employability skills—such as time management, speaking, and writing—most colleges in the region do not explicitly incorporate these into their oil and natural gas–related degree programs.** Time management, speaking, and writing skills are rarely included in coursework offered by departments tailored to students in the oil and natural gas industry. Fifty-one percent of employers sought workers with time-management skills, but only 6 percent of colleges focus on this skill as part of their oil and natural degree programs. Similarly, 50 percent of employers sought workers with speaking skills and 48 percent of employers sought workers with writing skills; however, 0 percent and 7 percent of colleges, respectively, focused on those skills as part of their oil and natural gas degree programs.
- **Though most colleges in the tristate region report supporting students getting jobs in specific occupations within the oil and natural gas industry, few have stackable credential programs.** Stackable credential programs increasingly are receiving attention from workforce development policymakers and practitioners because they allow workers to obtain occupation-specific knowledge and skills in an efficient, flexible structure and format. However, only 28 percent of oil and natural gas degree programs in the region reported providing them.
- **Less than half of courses aimed at future workers in the oil and natural gas industry use contextualized instruction**. Contextualized instruction uses occupational applications to teach basic academic skills (and vice versa) in such a way that the student learns both simultaneously. The majority of courses offered in oil and natural gas–related departments in the tristate region use contextualized instruction less than half of the time, with 12 percent of courses never using contextualized instruction.

- **The majority of employers do not communicate results of workforce planning with colleges.** It is important to document how well oil and gas employers in the tristate region assess their workforce needs and communicate those findings to the postsecondary education institutions tasked with providing the talent pool to fill those jobs in highest demand. Fifty-nine percent of the employers responded that they do not. Of those that do, 30 percent identify and forward job vacancies to local education providers, and 26 percent provide key information on jobs needs and future occupational demands: Both of these reflect the kind of information that schools need to develop programs and course work to best meet the needs of employers. Only 8 percent of employers forecast job vacancies and communicate that future demand to schools.
- **Few employers provide deep or continual instructional or curricular support to colleges.** Sixty-four percent of employers report that they do not offer any instructional support to colleges.
- **Most employers (55 percent) do not provide any material or fiscal support to colleges for workforce development.** Of those that do provide support, 17 percent of employers reported offering scholarships and another 17 percent reported providing supplies and materials for hands-on training. Very few employers provided any of the other options, such as cash support for low-income students; equipment for realistic, high-fidelity training; or laboratory centers to share space and equipment.
- **Both colleges and employers point to each other's unwillingness and lack of time as key barriers to partnering.** Our surveys asked employers and colleges to report barriers to partnerships. While there is no one barrier that the majority of school or employers point to, the barrier that receives the most responses from both colleges and employers is the lack of active outreach from the other. Twenty-two percent of employers report that a key barrier is the lack of outreach from education and training providers. Thirty-four percent of colleges report unwillingness of employers with whom to partner is a key barrier. The barrier that

received the most responses from college representatives, however, was the lack of staff time to partner with employers.

Recommendations

Ensuring that the supply of talent has the knowledge and skills to best meet the demands of the region's oil and gas–sector companies requires a deepening of the connections between the actors and institutions in the workforce development system. The following recommendations could help colleges be more responsive to the knowledge and skill requirements of high-priority occupations while helping employers be more flexible in the workforces they hire and more proactive in their engagements with local colleges. We also suggest policies that state and local governments could enact to foster a collaborative workforce development ecosystem.

Colleges need to adjust programming so that it fits better with the agile, flexible, and nonlinear nature of workforce development. The volatile nature of the oil and gas industry that results from fluctuations in supply and demand leaves employees particularly susceptible to shifts in employment (Gonzalez et al., 2017). Full-time long-term employment with a single employer is no longer the modal experience in the United States. Throughout their lives, American workers have stints with multiple employers interspersed with periods of training or retraining, unemployment, and job searching. However, our analyses revealed that the oil and gas workforce development system in the tristate region does not appear to support contemporary workers with dynamic and versatile careers. In our study, very few local colleges incorporate contextualized learning or stackable credentialing, both of which align better with the current dynamic nature of work. Including contextual-learning, stackable credentialing, or both to better fit the nature of employment in an evolving, technologically innovative sector is vital.

Colleges should prioritize the development of work-based learning opportunities for students, such as internships or cooperatives, which provide hands-on experiential learning at a worksite. Interviews with employers revealed that they are eager to work with colleges to offer work-based learning opportunities; they simply do not know whom to contact or how best to organize an agreement. Thus, college presidents or department heads will need to actively reach out to local employers to set up, standardize, and implement a sustainable and practical internship or other work-based learning program that is integrated within coursework. Incorporating work-based learning opportunities within coursework could have the added benefit of exposing students to a variety of jobs, which should improve career decisionmaking and could afford students vital on-the-job experience that our analyses found employers are looking for.

Employers will need to become more flexible in hiring and placement decisions to keep pace with the labor market's needs for an agile workforce. Our analyses revealed that the high-priority occupations in most demand required a minimum of five years of experience. But employers reported in interviews that they had difficulty finding the right types of workers to fill these jobs. Employers therefore have three options to ensure that high-priority occupations are filled: (1) Look for the nontraditional applicant who has moved across jobs and industries who has the years of experience and who could be "trained up" in the particular occupation, (2) develop their incumbent workers and improve their skills, or (3) offer opportunities for entry-level applicants to gain the knowledge and cross-cutting skills while on the job. None of these options are short-term fixes; they will require long-term planning.

In addition to community colleges and private training institutes, include four-year colleges and universities and other stakeholders, such as workforce investment boards and industry trade associations, in strategies for workforce development and planning. Though much attention has been paid to the development of subbaccalaureate programs that provide certificates, occupational licenses, and associate's degrees that are clearly required for middle-skill jobs, four-year colleges and universities should be part of the conversation. Our analysis finds that 88 percent of employers report having high-priority occupations that require a bachelor's degree. In crafting a broader workforce development system, we need to be mindful of the full array of occupations required to sustain a thriving regional oil and natural gas economy, not just those for unskilled entry-level employees.

Acknowledgments

We thank the National Science Foundation for its generous sponsorship of this research, and are particularly grateful to Earnestine Psalmonds Easter, program director of the Division of Graduate Education. We also thank Andrew Naber for developing the survey instruments; Alerk Amin, Karen Edwards, Zoltan Szalay, and Liz Voss for programming and administering the surveys; and Kyle Siler-Evans and Julia Kaufman for providing helpful feedback through the course of the project. We are also grateful to the Pennsylvania Independent Oil and Gas Association, the West Virginia Oil and Natural Gas Association, and the Ohio Oil and Gas Association for providing us access to their members to field our surveys. Finally, Mary Murrin of the Chevron Corporation made this project possible through her leadership in championing research on workforce development in the oil and natural gas industry. As part of RAND's quality assurance process, two unnamed peer reviewers provided constructive feedback that improved the overall quality of this report. M. Rebecca Kilburn coordinated RAND's quality assurance process for this project. Lastly, we are indebted to the employers and education and training providers who took the time to fill out our surveys and to answer our questions. Those responses and stories are the bedrock of our analysis, and it is our hope that the findings are useful to the respondents as they continue to contribute to economic growth and opportunities across the tristate region.

Abbreviations

KSAO	knowledge, skills, abilities, and other characteristics
MMIC	Multimode Interviewing Capability
O*NET	Occupational Information Network Data Collect Program
SHALE	Skills for a Healthy Agile Local Economy and Workforce
STEM	science, technology, engineering, and mathematics

CHAPTER ONE

Introduction

Following a period of slow growth, natural gas production in the United States grew by more than 25 percent from 2007 to 2013 (Hausman and Kellogg, 2015). Further, the industry anticipates 1.9 million job openings through 2035 (IHS Global Inc., 2016). This unprecedented expansion has rapidly changed the employment landscape in Ohio, Pennsylvania, and West Virginia (i.e., the "tristate" region). The Marcellus Shale and the Utica Shale, which collectively extend across the tristate region and into parts of New York and Maryland, is one of the largest U.S. gas fields ranked by estimated proved reserves (U.S. Energy Information Administration, 2017b). In the tristate region and across the country, the U.S. Department of Energy projects increased production, consumption, and prices of oil and natural gas for the coming decades (U.S. Energy Information Administration, 2017a).

This growth in the industry is occurring against the backdrop of an aging population of oil and natural gas workers who are now entering their retirement years (National Research Council, 2013). Coinciding with this industrywide expansion is a change in required skill levels: As manual skills become less valuable than the technological ones needed to operate the emerging forms of equipment that are characteristic of this sector (National Research Council, 2013), many workers with obsolete skills are being displaced. Such changes—expansion in the industry and an uptick in retirements—have created new challenges for employers, along with creating new opportunities for postsecondary institutions that provide education and training to the projected 1.9 million future oil and natural gas workers. The gap between employer needs and employee skills is widest in the near term, when more jobs will open up than the current output of graduates is likely to meet, retirements will increase among the baby-boomer generation (Center for Energy Workforce Development, undated), and reliance on technical skills in the workforce will continue to increase (National Research Council, 2013). With an expansion in the science, technology, engineering, and mathematics (STEM) economy and the growing demand for workers to fill STEM jobs, business leaders are putting pressure on—and in some cases, providing investments in—schools to recalibrate their curricula to emphasize STEM skills directly required on the job (Tai, 2012), particularly for those jobs specific to the energy sector and within the burgeoning oil and natural gas industry (National Research Council, 2013).

With such unprecedented growth to date and with further demand expected, ensuring that the industry has access to a prepared, skilled workforce is paramount to sustaining economic growth in the tristate region. What knowledge and skills are oil and natural gas employers looking for when trying to fill positions? To what extent is the local education system prepared to provide those knowledge areas and skills to their students, who are facing a rapidly changing job market characterized by technological innovation? How can employers and education and training providers work together more collaboratively and creatively to create clear career pathways out of the classroom and into the workplace? Answers to these questions are essential for employers, educators, policymakers, and other stakeholders to make informed investments in sustaining this industry as part of a broader regional economic development strategy.

Objectives of This Study

The RAND Corporation, a nonprofit, nonpartisan research institution with a regional office in the heart of the Marcellus and Utica shale regions (Pittsburgh, Pennsylvania), is committed to providing stakeholders in the oil and natural gas industry with rigorous, objective analyses that can help them make such investments. This report, produced by

RAND with support from the National Science Foundation, includes findings from our analysis of original data that are in the spirit of this mission. Specifically, this report empirically addresses three aims:

- Document the knowledge and skills required by employers in the oil and natural gas industry (Chapter Three).
- Assess the extent to which colleges are positioned to provide employers in the oil and natural gas industry with workers who have appropriate knowledge and skills for high-priority occupations (Chapter Four).
- Identify collaborative strategies and practices already in place that connect employers in the oil and natural gas industry with educators (Chapter Five).

Previous work has explored the demand for industry-specific knowledge and skills in the region, including official government industry projections (such as those available through the Bureau of Labor Statistics or state labor market and workforce analysis offices) and labor market forecasts that rely on data from federal surveys or job postings (e.g., Burning Glass Technologies, Council for Adult and Experiential Learning, and Allegheny Conference on Community Development, 2016; Lendel et al., 2015). But these studies tend to focus on specific localities (e.g., one state or one metropolitan area) or cast a wide net across multiple employment sectors, or they do not incorporate supply-side factors, such as the available skill set of a talent pool or the education and training opportunities available. Put simply, most analyses that document supply and demand in a region simply tabulate the number of jobs in the industry that are expected to need filling alongside the number of individuals living in the region who possess the levels of education required to perform those jobs, without examining how local employers and schools in the region interact and collaborate to sustain an optimal school-to-work pipeline. Our analysis fills this gap with quantitative and qualitative data collected directly from employers and educators on these collaborative efforts. In doing so, this study contributes new knowledge about the workforce development system that undergirds a growing and prosperous regional economy.

The remainder of this chapter provides context for our study. We first document educational requirements of projected new jobs in the oil and natural gas industry as background for understanding the scope of workforce development needs in the industry at the national level. We then describe the economic and postsecondary educational conditions in the tristate region, provide an overview of the workforce development system that has been established to support economic growth in the region, and explain the rationale for building a strong workforce development system in the region.

Educational Requirements for New Jobs in the Oil and Natural Gas Industry

As context for our study, we first highlight the educational requirements for new jobs in the oil and natural gas industry at the national level. To do so, we aggregated employment projections through 2024 as produced by the Bureau of Labor Statistics (undated-a) for occupations that compose the industry. A limitation of this approach is that occupations do not neatly map onto industries. For example, heavy and tractor-trailer truck drivers, which play a critical role in downstream segments of the industry, work across a number of industries, not just oil and natural gas. Because the Bureau of Labor Statistics does not parse occupation by industry, we cannot discern exactly how much of the educational demand for specific occupations can be directly attributable to new jobs created in the oil and natural gas industry. Therefore, these projections should be used to gauge broad trends in educational demands in the industry rather than specific quantities.[1]

---

[1] The Bureau of Labor Statistics only identifies the educational requirements needed for occupations, not for industries. To identify the occupations that make up the oil and natural gas industry, we used the National Academies of Science classification scheme for the 20 largest private-sector occupations in each of the different segments of the industry (National Research Council, 2013). As a handful of occupations occupy multiple segments (e.g., industrial machinery mechanics are a part of downstream and midstream segments of the industry), we show the findings by segment to avoid double counting of occupations.

In Figure 1.1 we show the percentage of job openings between 2014 and 2024 in the oil and natural gas industry that require education beyond high school—including bachelor's degrees, associate's degrees, and occupational certifications—for each of the three main segments of the industry: upstream (fossil, nuclear, wind, and solar energy production and extraction), midstream (transportation and distribution of energy via pipelines and newly developed integrative technologies), and downstream (refining of petroleum crude oil, processing and purifying of raw natural gas, and marketing and distribution of products derived from crude oil and natural gas into petrochemicals or plastics). In the downstream and midstream segments of the industry, the majority of jobs expected to need filling do not require education beyond high school. However, *a nonnegligible proportion of new jobs will require postsecondary education*—36 percent of new downstream jobs and 41 percent of new midstream jobs will need workers with

Figure 1.1
Postsecondary Educational Requirements of Projected Job Openings in the Oil and Natural Gas Industry from 2014 Through 2024, by Segment of the Industry

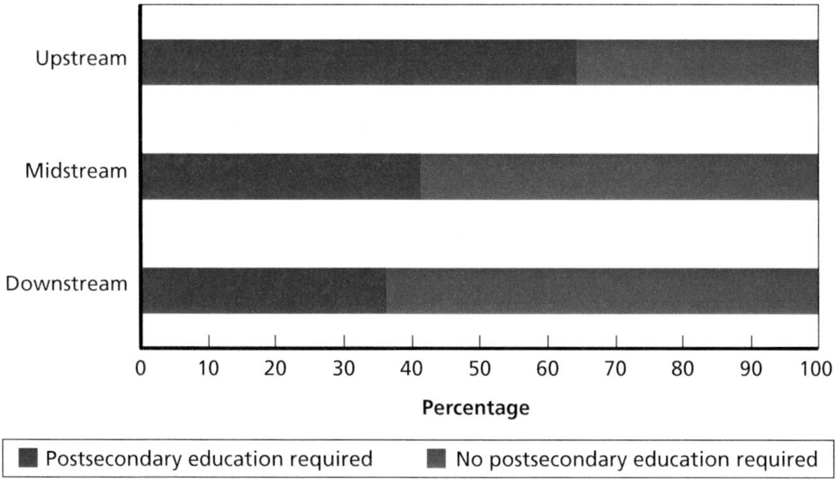

SOURCE: Authors' calculations based on data from U.S. Bureau of Labor Statistics (2016).

RAND *RR2199-1.1*

at least some education beyond high school. Moreover, the majority of new upstream jobs (64 percent) will require at least some education beyond high school. Projections indicate that the industry will require 1.4 million workers for upstream jobs, 350,000 for midstream jobs, and 30,000 for downstream jobs (IHS Global Inc., 2016). Therefore, effective workforce development strategies must consider how to utilize postsecondary training institutions to partly meet the demand expected in the industry over the coming years.

While recognizing the importance of a cohesive, aligned "K–16" (kindergarten through college) STEM school-to-workforce pipeline, our study focuses only on postsecondary institutions that provide training beyond a traditional high school degree. We do not examine career and technical education provided in high school settings or the foundational STEM curriculum implemented in local middle and elementary schools. Our rationale for focusing on postsecondary education (and by extension, jobs in the industry that require postsecondary education) is based on three reasons. First, at least a third of new jobs in the downstream and midstream segments of the industry and more than half of new jobs in the upstream segment (which is the largest segment) will require training beyond high school. Second, postsecondary institutions—including job-training programs and technical schools that require a high school diploma as a prerequisite—serve as critical portals that directly connect local school systems with employers. Postsecondary institutions are also increasingly involved in providing oil and gas–specific degree programs, which help take on some of the "burden" of providing job training. Unlike high schools, which have a broader academic and developmental mission, postsecondary institutions have more resources and latitude to create programs that can be tailored to specific occupations. Third, and finally, this study is part of a larger initiative in the region to inform the development of postsecondary programs that can best prepare students for jobs in the oil and natural gas industry. Consequently, we do not pay much attention in this report to jobs that require a high school diploma or less, or to the specific types of knowledge and skills needed to perform those jobs.

The Oil and Natural Gas Industry in the Tristate Region

While the tristate region already has well-established fossil fuel energy extraction and production, natural gas resources have further driven the development of the region's energy sector since 2011 (Gonzalez et al., 2016; Gonzalez et al., 2017). The region is also home to a burgeoning and varied energy economy in upstream, midstream, and downstream segments of the industry and to developers of innovations in smart building technologies and energy storage (Gonzalez et al., 2014; Gonzalez et al., 2015). The oil and natural gas industry, on which this report focuses, includes exploration drilling and preparation for shipment of crude petroleum and natural gas. As of May 2017, the industry accounts for more than $300 billion in revenue (U.S. Department of Labor, 2012). Two of the largest reserves of oil and natural gas in the country are the Utica and Marcellus shales (Figure 1.2), which received a boost in productivity thanks in part to the implementation of horizontal drilling and hydraulic fracturing technology. With this technology, the tristate region has experienced an elevated economic profile and activity, including a boom in the generation of tax revenue.[2]

In Ohio, hydrocarbon production has risen sharply over the past ten years. In 2005, the state produced 83 billion cubic feet of nat-

---

[2] States have adopted varying tax schemes and distribution strategies to be responsive to the new local output from the industry. In 2012, the Pennsylvania General Assembly enacted Act 13, which included changes to Pennsylvania's environmental laws overseeing shale gas development and authorized county governments to impose an impact fee paid annually by unconventional natural gas producers for each well they *spud*, or start to drill, each calendar year (Pennsylvania General Assembly, 2012). The impact fee and other taxes associated with the natural gas industry have generated more than $3.1 billion in revenue for the Commonwealth of Pennsylvania from 2012 to 2016 (Marcellus Shale Coalition, 2016). Ohio does not have an impact fee, but in 1973 instituted a severance tax of 3 cents per thousand cubic feet of natural gas and 20 cents per barrel of oil. There is no tax on natural gas liquids, including ethane, butane, and propane. Income from the severance tax jumped from $2.5 million in fiscal year 2010 to around $25 million in fiscal year 2015 (Policy Matters Ohio, 2017). West Virginia's severance tax is 4.7 cents per thousand cubic feet of natural gas. Counties in which there is direct natural gas extraction receive 75 percent of the severance tax; 25 percent is distributed to remaining counties. In fiscal year 2015, West Virginia accrued $58 million from the severance tax (West Virginia Department of Revenue, 2016).

Figure 1.2
Map of Utica and Marcellus Shale Region

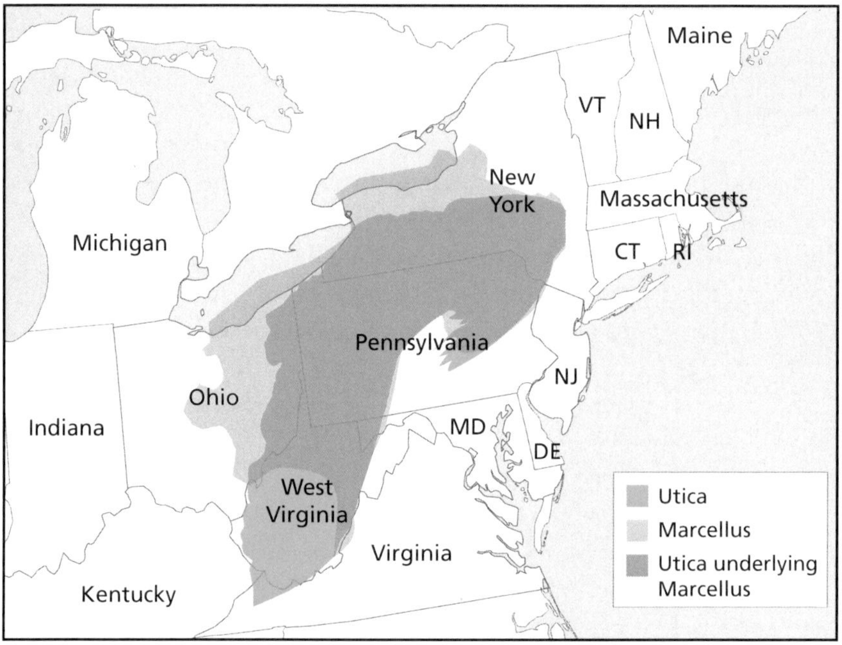

RAND *RR2199-1.2*

ural gas. By 2015, production had grown to 955 billion cubic feet, an increase of more than 1,000 percent (U.S. Energy Information Administration, 2016a). Additionally, Ohio stands as the largest oil producer in the region. According to the U.S. Department of Energy, state oil production peaked at 26 million barrels in 2015, reaching this level after dipping to a multi-decade low of 4.6 million barrels just four years prior (U.S. Energy Information Administration, 2016b). But Ohio energy production growth has not directly led to a spike in employment. In January 2005, 2,400 individuals were employed in the state's oil and natural gas extraction sector. In August 2012, sector employment peaked at 3,200. Since then, however, employment has fallen almost 50 percent, from 3,100 individuals to 1,650 individuals in 2016 (U.S. Bureau of Labor Statistics, undated-b).

Similar to Ohio, the oil and natural gas resources within Marcellus Shale transformed the energy profile of Pennsylvania (U.S. Energy Information Administration, 2016a). In 2005, the state produced 168 billion cubic feet of natural gas. By 2015, natural gas production grew to 4.8 trillion cubic feet, an increase of more than 2,700 percent. In that year, Pennsylvania accounted for almost 20 percent of total U.S. natural gas production. Increased output in natural gas was accompanied by steady growth in oil production. Continuing a trend that began in the late 1990s, oil production has grown by 5.6 million barrels—to a 2014 peak of 7 million barrels (U.S. Energy Information Administration, 2016b). Unlike in Ohio, increases in energy production did boost employment in Pennsylvania. In January 2005, 1,700 individuals were employed in the oil and natural gas extraction sector of Pennsylvania (U.S. Bureau of Labor Statistics, undated-b). By the end of the 2015, that number had grown to almost 6,600. Although oil gas extraction employment declined somewhat to just 5,400 jobs in 2016, this was still more than three times levels in 2005 (U.S. Bureau of Labor Statistics, undated-b).

Traditionally considered coal country, West Virginia has emerged as a major source of natural gas production. In 2005, the state produced 213 billion cubic feet of natural gas. By 2015, production levels had grown to 1.2 trillion cubic feet, an increase of more than 450 percent (U.S. Energy Information Administration, 2016a). Over a longer horizon, state oil production increased as well. From 2001 to 2016, West Virginia went from 1.2 million barrels to 8 million barrels, an increase of more than 500 percent (U.S. Energy Information Administration, 2016b). Similar to Pennsylvania, increases in West Virginia's oil and natural gas production were accompanied by significant increases in sector employment. In 2005, fewer than 1,900 individuals were employed in the sector. By 2014, sector employment had grown to more than 2,800. Although the year-over-year changes were not uniformly positive, the trend line points upward. As of 2016, annual employment in the industry was 24 percent above 2005 levels (U.S. Bureau of Labor Statistics, undated-b).

In using the states' oil and natural gas association rosters, we estimate there are approximately 730 firms operating in the oil and natural gas industry across the tristate region (30 in Ohio, 365 in Pennsylvania, and 23 in West Virginia, with the remainder headquartered in other states). Overall, the economies of Ohio, Pennsylvania, and West Virginia have benefited from increased activity in the oil and natural gas extraction sector. Ohio oil and gas sector gross domestic product (GDP) reached $5.1 billion in 2015, up from $1.2 billion in 2005. Likewise, Pennsylvania sector GDP totaled $9.8 billion in 2015, up from $570 million in 2005. Finally, West Virginia sector GDP totaled $3 billion in 2015, an increase over the 2005 level of $605 million (U.S. Bureau of Economic Analysis, 2017). Sustaining this growth in output will require attention to training new workers for large number of job openings expected in the industry.

The Educational Context of the Tristate Region

Employers depend on schools to provide a workforce with the knowledge and skills they need to fill jobs. The tristate region is home to a diverse collection of postsecondary educational and training institutions. These institutions include liberal arts colleges, such as Oberlin College, Dickinson College, and Bethany College; large state universities, such as Ohio State University, Pennsylvania State University, and the University of West Virginia; and community colleges, such as Cuyahoga Community College, Pennsylvania College, and Pierpont Community College. Altogether there are more than 500 degree- or certificate-bearing schools in the three states (National Center for Education Statistics, undated).

A high yield of college graduates requires that students first finish high school. Overall levels of high school diploma receipt for the three states are on par with the nation as a whole (U.S. Census Bureau, 2016). In 2015, 87 percent of adults held a high school diploma or equivalent nationally. Ohio and Pennsylvania were ahead of the national average at 89 percent while West Virginia lagged somewhat behind at 85 percent.

A different dynamic emerges for college completion rates. Whereas high school completion in Ohio and Pennsylvania are just above than the national average, college completion rates are just below it. In 2015,

30 percent of adults nationally held a bachelors' degree. For the same year, 26 and 29 percent of residents in Ohio and Pennsylvania, respectively, attained a bachelor's degree or more. West Virginia was much farther below the national average, at 19 percent (U.S. Census Bureau, 2016).

The oil and natural gas industry is particularly reliant on those graduating with STEM degrees (Baird, Bozick, and Harris, forthcoming in late 2017). The National Science Foundation directly tracks STEM degree completion by calculating the number of STEM degrees per 1,000 individuals. In 2011, there were 16.2 STEM degrees per 1,000 Ohio adult residents, 22.3 STEM degrees per 1,000 Pennsylvania adult residents, and 20.8 STEM degrees per 1,000 West Virginia adult residents. Respectively, the states rank 33rd, 10th, and 18th overall in the production of STEM degrees (National Science Foundation, 2011).

The Need for an Efficient, Effective, and Agile Sector-Based Workforce Development System in the Tristate Region

There is growing recognition that while the economy is global, responsibilities for economic growth are local, labor sheds are regional, and thus local talent and human capital are drivers of a community's economic vitality (National Academy of Sciences, Engineering, and Medicine, 2016). But colleges and education providers cannot act in a vacuum to support a region's economic vitality; rather, they must actively engage and partner with other stakeholders (Moretti, 2013)—especially when a substantial share of the job openings expected in the coming years will require workers with some postsecondary education. A variety of strategies have been developed to promote skill development and sustainable employment for regional workforces. Comprehensive and effective workforce development strategies typically incorporate a combination of partnerships among educational institutions (e.g., high schools, community colleges), regional employers, and government agencies (e.g., Workforce Development Boards). Promoting collaboration among these different stakeholders results in a comprehensive approach to workforce development that focuses on addressing multiple needs (e.g., labor shortages, unemployment, or national energy goals). One nationally recognized promising practice is the sector-based public-private model (King and Prince, 2015).

Sector-based public-private models are partnerships between public agencies and the economic stakeholders in a targeted industry, cluster of industries, or occupations. The partnership plans and implements customized education and training programs to upgrade the skills of the workforce and improve the economic performance of the region (Harper-Anderson, 2008; Kochan, Finegold, and Osterman, 2012). Sector-based models "seek to develop deep knowledge of the markets, technology, and labor market circumstances of the industry and, through this knowledge, to contribute to both the human resource and also the economic growth and development needs of the industry" (Osterman, 2007, p. 139). Thus, rather than one employer working with an education or training program to fill jobs, sector-based programs involve multiple employers (as well as trade associations and/or unions) in a region or industry sector that articulate their workforce and skills demands, and numerous education and training institutions—both private and public—working collectively to meet those employer needs. Because this approach targets an entire sector rather than a single company, a sector-based program may involve the government or public sector to help an entire sector become more competitive. These partnerships can act as vehicles to enhance student learning and performance in STEM fields and to diversify pathways to STEM careers (President's Council of Advisors on Science and Technology, 2012; National Science and Technology Council, 2013).

Indeed, a number of recent federal efforts are aimed at addressing these issues—each emphasizing that sector-based public-private partnerships are a potentially promising practice to develop a job-driven U.S. workforce and training system:

- In 2012, President Obama convened the President's Council on Jobs and Competitiveness, composed of 25 leaders from business, labor, and academia, to develop ideas to accelerate job growth and improve the country's long-term position in the global economy (Office of the Press Secretary, 2012).

- In July 2014, the White House released the report, *Ready-to-Work: Job-Driven Training and American Opportunity*, which endorsed "job-driven" training as a solution to issues facing the U.S. workforce system (Biden, 2014).
- On July 9, 2014, Congress passed the Workforce Innovation and Opportunity Act of 2014 (WIOA) (Public Law 113-128). This Act reauthorizes the Workforce Investment Act of 1998 (Public Law 105-220) and ties federal workforce training money to local and regional employers that will help customize training programs at high schools and community colleges. It also consolidates programs and provides more local flexibility in how they are run. The aim of this act is to promote workforce-development programs that are directly tied to skills demands. WIOA requires states to develop unified plans across all WIOA-authorized programs and encourages them to incorporate the White House's Job-Driven Checklist into their new plans.
- At the time of the writing of this report, Congress is set to renew the Carl D. Perkins Career and Technical Education Improvement Act, which provides federal funds to states to bolster their vocational education programs in high schools via connections with local industries.

Recognizing the importance of the oil and natural gas industry in the region and the role that a job-driven workforce development system could take in supporting the region's economic development, state leaders in Ohio, Pennsylvania, and West Virginia have worked with institutions of higher education, industry leaders, and nonprofit organizations to develop cross-state cooperation related to the education and workforce development in the energy sector. For example, in 2014, Chevron Corporation established the Appalachia Partnership Initiative, a network of partner organizations from the business, foundation, nonprofit, research, and education sectors. The goals of the Appalachia Partnership Initiative are to strengthen STEM education in middle and high schools and to improve pathways for high school graduates and adult learners to careers in the oil and gas industries and in advanced manufacturing. In addition to Chevron Corporation, partners include an employer membership nonprofit, the Allegheny Conference on Community Development; two philanthropic foundations, the Claude Worthington Benedum Foundation and the Grable Foundation; and a manufacturing extension partnership, Catalyst Connection ("Appalachia Partnership Initiative," undated).

As a second example, the Benedum Foundation initiated an effort in 2015 to connect 32 counties in Ohio, Pennsylvania, and West Virginia—engaging thousands of citizens across the counties in town hall meetings and convening leaders in business, government, and philanthropy. With a leadership board consisting of government officials and private-sector industry leaders, the foundation's goal is to implement 15 initiatives covering six domains—economy, education, environment, community and people, government, and transportation and infrastructure—to unlock the potential of the region and improve its future (Pittsburgh Foundation, undated).

A third example of collaborative relationship-building in the tristate region was the 2015 signing of the Tri-State Shale Agreement by the governors of Ohio, Pennsylvania, and West Virginia (Tri-State Shale Coalition, undated). That agreement set the stage for the Tri-State Shale Coalition, which was formed to unite key stakeholders involved in the economic development of the areas affected by the Marcellus and Utica shale plays in Ohio, Pennsylvania, and West Virginia.

Fourth, a consortium of four colleges in the region—Stark State College (Ohio), Westmoreland County Community College and Pennsylvania College of Technology (Pennsylvania), and Pierpont Community and Technical College (West Virginia)—received Department of Labor funding from 2011 through 2016 to work collaboratively with each other and local employers to stand up a new program, ShaleNET, which offers stackable credentials for high-priority occupations in the oil and natural gas industry. The U.S. Department of Labor defines stackable credentials as those that are "part of a sequence of credentials that can be accumulated over time and move an individual along a career pathway or up a career ladder" (U.S. Department of Labor, 2012). The credentials are stackable in that you can acquire a certification on which you can later "stack" additional credits that count toward another certification or degree. Combined, these stackable credential programs have reached more than 1,200 students, exposing them to hands-on training and career counseling, and nearly three-quarters of graduates were employed following completion of the program (Dunham et al., 2016). The ShaleNET consortium serves as regional model for sector-driven workforce development, with efforts currently under way to scale up and expand. The findings from this report are intended in part to inform the maintenance and expansion of the consortium, given its members' roles as collaborators in the Appalachia Partnership Initiative that supports ShaleNET.

Although the tristate region has a history of public-private collaboration, a number of challenges remain. First, collaborative efforts have been relatively disparate to date: working on separate activities with different goals. Second, the region is experiencing a shortfall in working-age population and skilled human capital in STEM fields—due to both retirements and lack of a growing population base (Burning Glass Technologies, Council for Adult and Experiential Learning, and Allegheny Conference on Community Development, 2016)—which can exacerbate the problem of trying to fill jobs in the oil and natural gas sector with workers who possess the right level of experience, knowledge, and skills. Third, while the political will to work collaboratively across state lines exists, the reality is that each state is governed by separate regulations and state legislatures, which need to be considered when developing any kind of tristate collaboration or effort. This report can help inform the direction of these collaborations so that they can effectively utilize the relationships and resources already in place in the region. It will also show how an effective and comprehensive sector-based public-private partnership could operate in the region.

Organization of This Report

Chapter Two details the data and methods we used to undertake our analysis. Chapters Three through Five presents our findings with respect to our research aims listed above. Finally, the report concludes in Chapter Five with recommendations on how the region's stakeholders can strengthen the oil and gas workforce development system.

CHAPTER TWO

Data Sources

To address our three research aims, we draw on three original data sources: a survey we designed and administered to oil and natural gas employers in the tristate region (The RAND SHALE Survey of Employers), a survey we administered to colleges and universities in the tristate region (The RAND SHALE Survey of Educators and Training Institutes), and data from interviews we conducted with a purposive sample of oil and natural gas employers in the tristate region. We describe these sources in turn.

The RAND SHALE Survey of Employers

The RAND SHALE (Skills for a Healthy Agile Local Economy and Workforce) Survey of Employers was designed to provide a representative portrait of the knowledge and skills needs of employers in the tristate region. To undertake this survey, we developed a population frame that included business representatives identified through professional association rosters and the Department of Labor (Career One Stop, undated). The professional organizations we utilized were the the Ohio Oil and Gas Association, the Pennsylvania Independent Oil and Gas Association, the West Virginia Oil and Natural Gas Association. Each association provided a roster of its membership. The rosters included the company name, company contact, and email address, but every listing was not complete and may not have contained information for every field. The rosters also included data fields for company type. For instance, distinctions were made between energy producers and contracted service providers. Rosters also included listings for professional firms, including accounting, real estate, insurance, and law. These firms were not involved in the technical extraction or movement of minerals but were most likely members of the association because of their expertise in the legal and financial sectors supporting the oil and natural gas industry. In total, these professional associations provided more than 700 listings of oil and gas extraction companies.

Concurrent with the identification and organization of the sample population, we developed the employer survey instrument. To create the survey instrument, we first identified high-priority occupations in the oil and gas industry sector. Recruitment for these occupations is the survey's basis of inquiry. The high-priority occupations used in the employer survey were selected by reviewing existing literature (Gonzales et al., 2014; Gonzales et al., 2015; Gonzales et al., 2016; Gonzales et al., 2017) and U.S. Department of Labor categorizations for industries and occupations (U.S. Census Bureau, undated). We also relied on the U.S. Department of Labor Employment and Training Administration's Occupational Information Network Data Collect Program (O*NET) Resource Center. O*NET is a repository of occupational information and analysis derived from surveys of workers and employers on the type of knowledge, skills, abilities, and other characteristics (KSAOs) required for specific occupations.[1] We then used the O*NET data to identify the KSAOs relevant to the oil and natural gas industry, which were then listed as response options on the survey. Third,

1 For example, welders are expected to have knowledge in basic mathematics, production, and processing; skills in critical thinking and monitoring; and abilities in control precision and problem sensitivity (O*Net, 2016).

we consulted workforce training and partnership literature, including industry technical reports, to determine both best practices for workforce development initiatives organized by public-private partnerships and common human resources practices. A substantial portion of the employer survey explores the arrangement of formal relationships between employers and educators in the oil and natural gas industry. To determine specific forms of education and training required for the high-priority occupations reported by employers on the survey, we applied the O*NET taxonomy.

We used a specialized unit within RAND to administer the employer and educator surveys. Multimode Interviewing Capability (MMIC) is a unit within RAND with demonstrated expertise in administering medium to large-scale surveys through an electronic platform while also implementing measures that protect the confidentiality of respondents. After MMIC received the population frame, it applied alphanumeric identifiers to each company. A linking file was created to include the identifiers and contact information of the entries. Respondents were invited to participate in the survey using their created identifier. As companies responded to the survey, their responses were collected under the assigned identifier. Throughout the administration of the survey, identifiers were reassigned to new companies. These reassignments were either prompted by feedback from invited survey participants or based on edits to contact information.

Respondents were invited between May and September of 2016 via email to participate in the survey. The email contained a link to the survey that included instructions and a description of the survey's inquiry and purpose. The email also included information on how respondents could contact a RAND team member to request extra guidance or concerns. Once a week, the team sent reminders to survey respondents. The team tailored messages to respondents who had started but not completed the survey, while the rest of the pool received a reminder about the general invitation. A few weeks into the administration of the survey, the team decided to incentivize participation with a small financial gift—first at a level of $10 per respondent, then increasing to $20 per respondent.

The membership list from the Ohio Oil and Gas Association had a number of missing and incorrect email addresses, which compromised our outreach efforts to oil and gas companies in that state. We were therefore only able to secure a survey from one employer in Ohio. The final sample includes 67 employers out of a total of 723 contacted for a response rate of 9 percent.[2] The final sample includes the one employer from Ohio, 50 employers from Pennsylvania, and 16 from West Virginia. Of the 67 employers, two were downstream industries, five were midstream, 26 were upstream, and 34 were either a mix of streams or support firms.[3]

So that results can approximately generalize to the population of employers in the tristate region, we created sampling weights that adjust all analyses included in this report for the "stream" of the industry, the size of the employer, and its geographic location. Because only a single Ohio employer responded, we assigned that respondent a weight at the mean rather than assigning an inflated weight that could force that single employer to represent all oil and natural gas firms in the state and potentially yield undue influence on our results. While we have no reason to believe that Ohio employers are substantively different from their peers in Pennsylvania and West Virginia, readers should note that our findings are largely reflective of employers in those latter states.

---

[2] During the administration of both the employer and education and training institute surveys, the project team closely monitored the level of participation and response rates of the targeted populations. The team used an online platform that allowed for 24-hour access to the survey over multiple months. However, we believe several factors attenuated our efforts, contributing to lower response rates than desired. First, the email invitation system made it easy to label our messages as spam or junk email. Second, we believe large segments of our targeted population were predisposed to be unwilling to participate in government-funded studies such as ours. Notably, when we called nonrespondents to remind them about the survey, employers indicated an unwillingness to discuss business practices with "outsiders."

[3] RAND analysts categorized each firm in the population frame by number of employees and "stream" using data on companies' characteristics from LexisNexis. It is worth noting that relative size of the streams in our sample (upstream as the largest; downstream as the smallest) accords with the national distribution of these streams across firms in the industry (National Research Council, 2013).

The RAND SHALE Survey of Education and Training Institutes

The RAND SHALE Survey of Education and Training Institutes was designed to provide a representative portrait of educational opportunities for students in the tristate region seeking training for employment in the oil and natural gas industry. This survey was developed and administered in parallel with the survey of employers described above. For this survey, we developed a population frame that included all postsecondary academic and training institutions in the three states that offer degrees at undergraduate level, associate's degrees, or certificates and offer programs or majors in at least one of the following areas:

- engineering
- physical sciences
- construction trades
- computer and information sciences and support services
- mechanic and repair technologies/technicians
- engineering technology and engineering-related fields
- science technology/technicians
- precision production
- transportation and materials moving.

Disciplines were chosen based on the nature and content of coursework, knowledge areas, and skills instructed or assessed while in program. Schools were identified from the U.S. Department of Education's Integrated Postsecondary Education Data System (IPEDS). We augmented schools identified from IPEDS with union-sponsored training institutes. These union establishments offer instruction for entry-level positions but do not necessarily offer widely accredited degrees. The unions were selected based on their composition and stated purposes related to the energy, manufacturing, or STEM trades. After the list of schools and unions were compiled, the team researched the names and email addresses of department chairs, instructors, or administrators within the departments.

The education and training institute survey was developed and administered using MMIC in parallel with the employer survey. Where it made sense to do so, we asked the same questions of educators as we did of employers to permit strategic comparisons. The survey was fielded via email between May and September of 2016. The final sample includes 87 schools out of a total of 436 contacted, for a response rate of 21 percent. The final sample included 42 schools from Ohio, 32 schools from Pennsylvania, and 13 schools from West Virginia. Of the 87 schools, 42 were four-year schools and 45 were less than four-year schools. So that our results can approximately generalize to the population of postsecondary education training providers in the tristate region, we created sampling weights that adjust all analyses included in this report for the type of school (four-year/less than four-year), the size of the student body, and its geographic location.

Interviews with Purposefully Selected Employers

In spring 2017, RAND researchers purposefully selected 30 oil and gas employers across the three states, pulling from the SHALE survey population rosters. We selected employers based on their state (Ohio, Pennsylvania, or West Virginia) and which "stream" the firm was categorized as (upstream, midstream, downstream, or mixed). Over the course of three months, we reached out to the selected employers via email and over the phone to invite them to participate in a 30-minute interview, offering a $25 gift card in appreciation for their time. In total, we sent three email invitations and called nonrespondents up to five times. Three employers had disconnected phone numbers and/or inactive email addresses or had closed operations; six employers declined to participate (one of whom was a no-show at the scheduled interview time and was unresponsive to efforts to reschedule); 15 employers did not return phone calls or emails. Our final sample included six firms (two upstream, two midstream, and two downstream; all located in Pennsylvania).

Interview questions mirrored the SHALE survey but inquired more deeply about employers' hiring practices, the types of knowledge and skills needed for high-priority occupations, how the firms assess applicants for those skills, the types of on-the-job training and career development opportunities provided to employees, and the types of partnerships and collaborations the firms have with education and training providers. The interview protocol is available in the Appendix.

Limitations of Analyses

Before turning to our findings, we want to draw readers' attention to three limitations of our analysis. First, our analysis is based on data collected directly from employers and educators, rather than traditional data sources used to construct population and employment projections. In talking directly to employers and college officials, we are able to ascertain detailed information about their organizations, their workers or students, and the extent of their collaborations, along with challenges and opportunities they face as actors in a regional workforce system. This in-depth information, which goes beyond standard population and employment projections, allows us to discern key components and processes within the system that can be improved. However, employers and colleges vary greatly in size and "reach" across the region, so direct comparisons of demand (in the form of responses supplied by representatives of firms) and supply (in the form of responses supplied by chairs of oil and natural gas–related degree programs at colleges) cannot be used to quantify movement through the school-to-work pipeline (i.e., a set number of schools need to do "Y" to effectively meet the demands of "Z" number of employers). We can only offer guidance about the salience of observed trends across employers and colleges, not specific projections.

Second, we were unable to effectively recruit the participation of Ohio employers in our survey. Consequently, our analysis of employers does not directly represent the needs of firms in the Buckeye State. Again, while Ohio employers are probably not substantively different from their peers in Pennsylvania and West Virginia, readers should note that our findings stem largely from employers in those latter states.

Finally, response rates to our surveys—9 percent for our survey of employers and 21 percent for our survey of education and training providers—were not as high as we had hoped. Our final samples span an array of employer types (upstream, midstream, downstream) and institution types (four-year, two-year, less than two-year), and we use sampling weights to adjust the estimates to generalize to the broader population of employers and schools. However, readers should keep in mind that our findings are based on a limited subset of these employers and schools. With these three caveats in mind, we present our findings in the following chapters.

CHAPTER THREE

Jobs and Skills in Demand: What Employers Need

It is vital to document the types of jobs and skills that are in highest demand for oil and gas companies in the region in order to ascertain the policies, practices, or initiatives that could be implemented to enhance prospective employees' employability. Using the results from the SHALE Survey of Employers, this chapter summarizes RAND's analyses of the characteristics of high-priority occupations that employers in the oil and natural gas industry in the tristate region reported their companies have: education levels or degrees, on-the-job training, or prior work experience that is required for an employee to have competence in that occupation. This chapter also describes the expected knowledge and skills required of those seeking employment in those occupations. We illuminate key findings with selected quotes from RAND's in-depth interviews with purposefully selected employers.

In our survey, we first asked employers to indicate high-priority occupations within their companies. The survey defined *high-priority occupations* as jobs that are in high demand, are critical to the company's core business, require more-advanced skills (education beyond high school), and provide family-sustaining wages. We use these occupations as an anchor for analysis. Figure 3.1 shows the distribution of these high-priority occupations as reported by survey respondents, organized from most prevalent to least prevalent. The top three most prevalent high-priority occupations reported by oil and natural gas employers in the survey were top executives (43 percent), engineers (41 percent), physical scientists, and construction trade workers (tied at 22 percent). We remind readers that although these occupations are

Figure 3.1
Percentage of Employers Reporting High-Priority Occupations

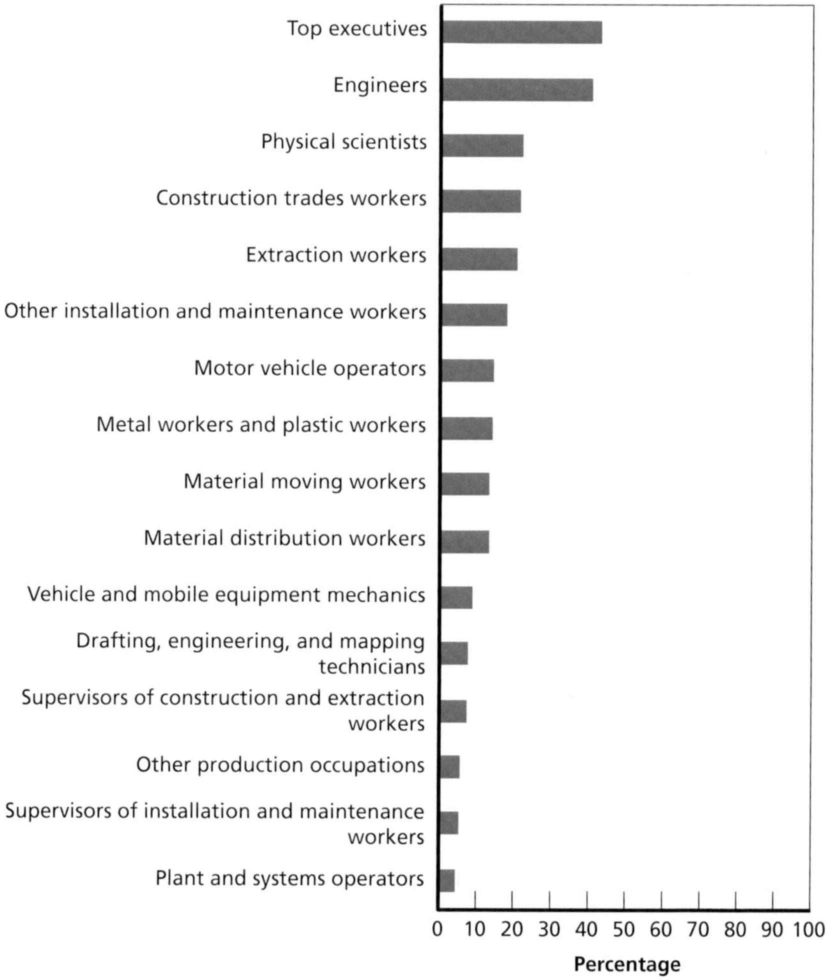

SOURCE: Authors' calculations using RAND SHALE Survey of Employers (2016–2017).
NOTE: N = 67. Results are weighted to generalize to all oil and natural gas employers in Pennsylvania and West Virginia. Responses do not add to 100 percent because respondents were allowed to mark multiple high-priority occupations.
RAND *RR2199-3.1*

viewed as *high priority* by employers, they may not necessarily be those in *most demand*. For example, most firms likely have multiple engineers and scientists, but far fewer top executives. Our survey does not access the specific number of engineers, scientists, and top executives needed by employers.

This suggests that within the oil and natural gas industry, there is heterogeneity in the occupational mix of different firms and/or differential valuation of these occupations across firms from the view of employers. There is not a single job or a set of jobs that is of high priority to most employers in the industry. This heterogeneity should be taken into consideration when attempting to develop systemwide recommendations for enhancing skills development.

Indeed, the interviews with our purposefully selected sample of oil and gas employers corroborate the variety in types of high-priority occupations in demand in the region: high-priority occupations varied based on whether the employer was in an upstream, midstream, or downstream industry. For example, high-priority occupations included lease operators (also known as well tenders), equipment operators, maintenance and service technicians, and electrical engineers in upstream companies; welders, pipeline layers, and commercial drivers in midstream companies; and occupations typical in processing (those handling the raw natural gas and ethanol coming through their systems and then moving a finished product out to distributors) such as machinists or warehouse operators in downstream companies. Each company representative also noted the demand for "desk jobs"—such as accountants, project managers, and supervisors.

Occupations Deemed High Priority by Employers Typically Require a Bachelor's Degree

Figure 3.2 shows the variation in levels of education needed for the high-priority occupations reported by employers listed in Figure 3.1; these analyses allow us to better understand the types of degrees that job seekers can pursue in attempting to meet the reported employment needs in the tristate region's oil and gas industry. We classified the

Figure 3.2
Percentage of Employers with High-Priority Occupations That Require Specific Levels of Education

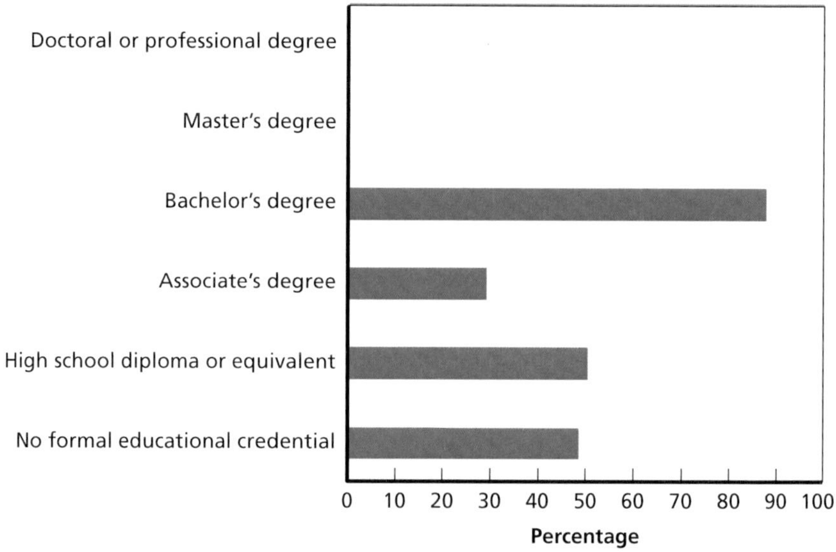

SOURCE: Authors' calculations using RAND SHALE Survey of Employers (2016–2017) and O*NET Resource Center (undated).
NOTE: N = 67. Results are weighted to generalize to all oil and natural gas employers in Pennsylvania and West Virginia. Responses do not add to 100 percent because respondents were allowed to mark multiple high-priority occupations.
RAND *RR2199-3.2*

education levels typically required for employment within each high-priority occupation listed in Figure 3.1 using the U.S. Department of Labor Employment and Training Administration O*NET survey codes (hereafter "O*NET"). Note that because employers could list multiple high-priority occupations, the combined percentages exceed 100. The values in the Figure can be interpreted as the percentage of employers whose stated high-priority occupations that require a particular level of education.

Figure 3.2 clearly illustrates that the lion's share of employers (88 percent) have high-priority occupations that require a bachelor's degree. Though sub-baccalaureate degrees, certifications, and licenses have attracted much attention in the oil and natural gas industry as stepping-stones into entry-level jobs, the hiring needs of employers in the region for their stated high-priority occupations broadly reflect demand for workers with bachelor's degrees. Note that there are no bars for post-baccalaureate degrees on the figure, as none of the high-priority jobs listed by employers required such degrees. The top three most-reported high-priority occupations listed in Figure 3.1—top executives, engineers, and physical scientists—require a bachelor's degree.[1]

Most of our interviewees noted that the level of education required for high-priority occupations within their companies depended on the occupation; some required postsecondary training, such as apprenticeships and certifications, but none required an advanced degree. For example, one interviewee from a pipelaying company noted that all that company's employees were union workers; thus, they had gone through an intensive apprenticeship and training program to become welders and did not require a specific advanced degree beyond what the union provides.

Another interviewee, from an energy production company, commented on how typical jobs in oil and gas require training beyond high school:

> . . . Folks should have basic understanding of the operations of an oil and gas well. There are a number of trade schools and technical colleges that are offering programs that prepare people for those positions. So it's not necessarily a college degree, but a technical degree or some level of experience: To be knowledgeable in other areas like welding or plumbing is also very useful. Those are very competitive positions, and we have a considerable number of applicants when we have a position available. And there is some turnover so those occur fairly frequently . . . There is an emphasis on environmental health and safety, and air emissions, in oil and

---

[1] As a reminder, when we asked employers to list their high-priority occupations, we defined these occupations specifically as those that require some education beyond high school. Given the phrasing of the question, we anticipated that most of the responses would include associate's degrees, bachelor's degrees, and other advanced degrees. That a sizable number of the reported high-priority occupations require only a high school degree or less (based on O*NET's classification) suggests that some employers have higher expectations for the education and training backgrounds of their employees who undertake these occupations.

> gas. We have people here with a master's degree and advanced degrees because that's the nature of the job market; those are the people available. But we really only need people with a bachelor's degree if they know about air, air emissions, or are coming from a basic engineering program.

Nearly a Quarter of Employers Reported Their Companies Had High-Priority Occupations That Require Long-Term On-the-Job Training

Improving the workforce development system in the region requires understanding the extent to which employers will need to supplement pre-employment education with job-specific training. A job applicant's degree or education level is typically viewed by employers as a "fixed trait" that could be augmented or enhanced with company- or position-specific knowledge, skills, and abilities to ensure an employee's competency. Such training requires an investment on the part of the employer, as many elements of jobs and their corresponding duties are not directly taught in the classroom—even in occupationally focused courses/degree programs. To quantify employers' need to supplement pre-employment education with on-the-job training, we classified the high-priority occupations reported in Figure 3.1 according to O*NET's taxonomy of the level of additional training needed to obtain competency on the job. The results are presented in Figure 3.3. Per O*NET definitions, *short-term* refers to a training program that is one month or less, *moderate-term* refers to a training program is more than one month and up to 12 months, and *long-term* refers to a training program that is longer than 12 months. Apprenticeships are the most intensive form of on-the-job training and can take up to two years or more depending on the specific job.

Eighty-eight percent of employers reported that their company had high-priority occupations that, according to O*NET, do not require on-the-job training. This indicates that many high-priority occupations in the industry do not necessitate special action on the part of employers to ensure that workers are integrated into the job.

Figure 3.3
Percentage of Employers with High-Priority Occupations That Require Specific Levels of On-the-Job Training Needed to Obtain Competency in High-Priority Occupations

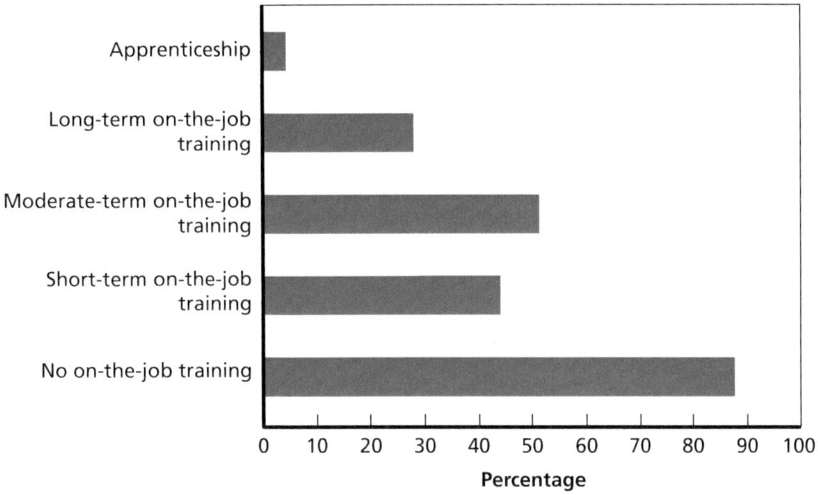

SOURCE: Authors' calculations using RAND SHALE Survey of Employers (2016–2017) and U.S. Department of Labor Employment and Training Administration O*NET Survey.
NOTE: N = 67. Results are weighted to generalize to all oil and natural gas employers in Pennsylvania and West Virginia. Responses do not add to 100 percent because respondents were allowed to mark multiple high-priority occupations.
RAND *RR2199-3.3*

However, there are still a number of occupations listed by employers that require moderate- or long-term training for workers to achieve competency in their position. About half of employers (52 percent) reported having high-priority occupations that require moderate-term on-the-job training (including inspectors, welders, and roustabouts) and about one in four employers (28 percent) reported having high-priority occupations that require long-term on-the-job training (including mechanics, machinists, and wellhead plumbers). Thus, for many of the oil and gas sector employers in the tristate region, it is essential to invest in and commit to providing on-the-job training to ensure their workers can adequately perform their duties.

The content of required on-the-job training varied among the companies we interviewed. All companies provided a basic safety training course; this was particularly salient in the pipelaying company, which had inspectors test all the welders before they could go into the field because "a high-pressure gas line is different from a water line." Other companies provided ongoing safety trainings at specific intervals (such as monthly or biweekly) that are related to a specific task, department-specific, or required by the Occupational Safety and Health Administration. These included such examples as first aid, cardiopulmonary resuscitation (CPR), defensive driving, and how to work in confined spaces or with hazardous materials.

Across the companies we interviewed, new hires experienced different levels of onboarding, depending on the department or task. One upstream company requires a yearlong training program for new hires. The first month is focused on safety, then the new hire is in a "trial period for several months where they are getting paid, but are shadowing different employees to get an understanding of the processes."

Another upstream company's onboarding was to require

> . . . abbreviated formal classes every two weeks, such as technology classes where we teach them about the technology used across the organization. [The training] is not just role specific, but also about intercompany communications, awareness of health safety and environmental training . . . and there are also department specific tasks they learn about, like how to operate a forklift, monitor different instruments in a plant, depending on their job.

All but one of the interviewees reported that their companies offer tuition reimbursement or opportunities. One company has a human resource policy to invest $10,000 for each employee in training, safety, or different certifications to ensure that the employees and the company abide by Environmental Protection Agency, the Occupational Safety and Health Administration, and state regulations. The company that does not have a formal tuition reimbursement policy pays for short courses or conferences directly, depending on the employee's need. For this company, the courses are typically for leadership training or strategic marketing, or a one-day training organized by a state oil and gas association.

The interviewee for that company commented:

> . . . we do occasionally pay for conferences out of office if it's specific to a task and very related to what someone is doing. So we're not generally going to send someone to DUG East for several thousand dollars, but if there was—last month, there was a very specific waste program put on by PIOGA [Pennsylvania Independent Oil and Gas Association]. It was a four- to five-hour training, and we did send individuals to that.

More Than Half of Employers Have High-Priority Occupations That Require at Least Five Years of Previous Work Experience

A key signal that applicants provide to prospective employers about their fit for the job is their previous work experience. Some employers have jobs that require years of experience to perform successfully, while others have jobs that can be performed by those brand new to the industry. To understand this variation in the context of the tristate oil and natural gas industry, we classified employers' stated high-priority occupations in terms of the amount of experience required for competency in that occupation, using O*NET's taxonomy of experience. *Experience* here refers to relevant work experience in a similar job and not necessarily experience in the same firm. We found that respondents employ three types of high-priority occupations: those that require no previous work experience (which tend to draw from new entrants to the labor market); those that require less than five years of work experience (which tend to draw from younger workers who have been out school for a few years); and those that require at least five years of work experience (which tend to draw from more-experienced workers). Figure 3.4 presents these results.

We found that 88 percent of respondents noted that at least some of their companies' high-priority occupations require no previous work

Figure 3.4
Percentage of Employers with High-Priority Occupations That Require Previous Work Experience for Desired Competency

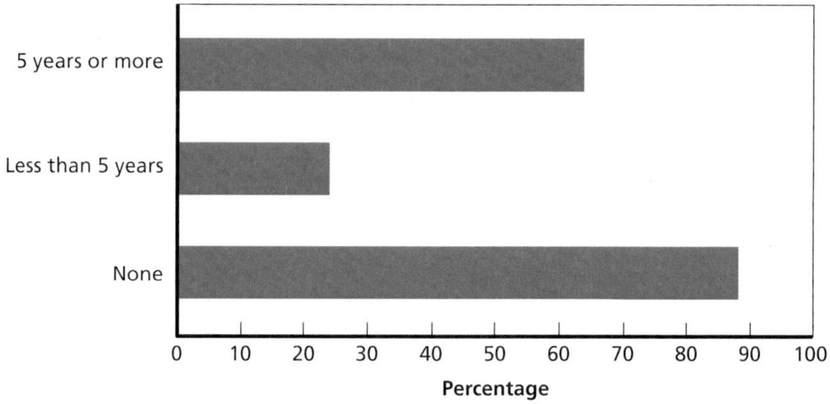

SOURCE: Authors' calculations using RAND SHALE Survey of Employers (2016–2017).
NOTE: N = 67. Results are weighted to generalize to all oil and natural gas employers in Pennsylvania and West Virginia. Responses do not add to 100 percent because respondents were allowed to mark multiple workforce planning activities.
RAND *RR2199-3.4*

experience; 64 percent reported that high-priority occupations in their companies require at least five years of previous work experience. This bimodal distribution suggests two distinct scenarios for employers. For a large swath of occupations, little will be expected of workers prior to their start. This should ease some of the pressure on prospective employees, as the "bar is low" with respect to the depth of their resumes. On the other end of the spectrum, a substantial proportion of employers have jobs that are best suited for those who have been in the labor market for some time—either within their own firm or outside of it. Both scenarios suggest that on-the-job training is paramount to workers' success. For employers filling positions that require no previous work experience, even the least-skilled jobs will require some form of training to teach workers how to do their jobs and how to function more broadly within the firm. For employers filling positions that require at least five years of work experience, the options are either to poach from competitors to secure already-trained talent or to provide their own ongoing training and professional development opportunities to groom young workers for more-advanced positions. Poaching is more cost-effective, but the provision of internal training opportunities and professional development create stronger internal integration, trust, and efficiency, resulting in greater worker productivity and company profitability.[2]

Interviewees noted this duality: High-priority occupations at the entry level did not require prior work experience. However, employers would prefer to hire someone with experience because that demonstrated an understanding of the nature of the work and how difficult it could be. For jobs that required more than a few years of education, finding someone with prior work experience was valuable. An interviewee from an upstream company noted that the high-priority occupations requiring a bachelor's degree typically also require someone with "a lot of experience; these are not entry-level jobs. The [new hires] come from other companies, such as a consultant or oil and gas company." For that same company, the interviewee noted,

> Oil and gas, and the regulations around air emissions, is so complicated that it's not something that you really pick up without experience, so a lot of the people that are getting the higher-paid jobs are coming either from consultants or other companies. So it's not an entry-level position.

Employers Seek Workers with Cross-Cutting Knowledge Areas and Skills

Regardless of whether workers filling high-priority occupations come from within or outside the company, employers will be evaluating candidates, making staffing decisions, and conducting business planning with an eye toward the knowledge and skills of their current and future employees. What exactly are employers looking for in their workers, and how do they determine whether applicants and/or current employees have what they are looking for? To address this question, the SHALE

---

2 See Lerman (2015) for a discussion.

Survey asked employers to identify the specific forms of knowledge and what types of skills they seek when filling positions for their high-priority occupations. To structure our analysis, we use the U.S. Department of Labor's Employment and Training Administration's conceptualization of knowledge and skills where knowledge represents the acquisition of facts and principles about a domain of information, whereas skills are the procedures to work with given knowledge (Reeder and Tsacoumis, 2017a; 2017b).

Administration and Management in Addition to Engineering and Technology Were Reported as Key Knowledge Areas

The three most highly sought types of knowledge for high-priority occupations, as reported by employers, were administration and management, engineering and technology, and computers and electronics (Figure 3.5). The most widely expressed need was for workers with knowledge of administration and management, reported by 55 percent of respondents. Administration and management is not specific to the oil and natural gas industry. Rarely is an understanding of effective management practices included in typical STEM curricula, be they STEM programs in high schools, community colleges, or four-year colleges. This does not necessarily mean that the largest group of jobs require knowledge of administration and management—firms could have a very small number of such jobs—but it does indicate that this is a form of knowledge needed by employers in the industry. Thus, it is worth considering how foundations of administration and management can be incorporated or emphasized in on-the-job training and other forms of professional development. That administration and management rises to the top of the list above more occupationally focused forms of knowledge suggests that workforce development strategies for this industry need to be reframed in terms of knowledge that might be *cross-cutting* rather than *job-specific*.

It is worth noting that engineering and technology remains a salient, essential form of knowledge for workers in the oil and natural gas industry (and was reported by 49 percent of employers in our survey). This is not surprising, given the nature of the work in the indus-

Figure 3.5
Percentage of Employers Reporting Types of Knowledge Needed for High-Priority Occupations

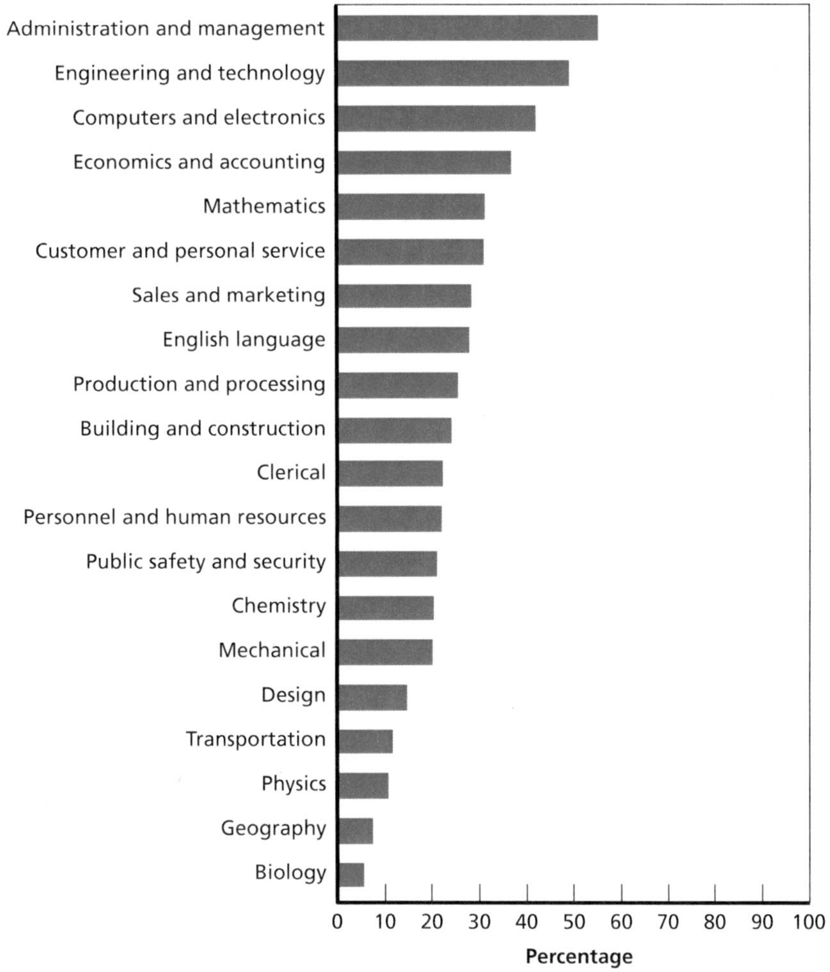

SOURCE: Authors' calculations using RAND SHALE Survey of Employers (2016–2017).
NOTE: N = 67. Results are weighted to generalize to all oil and natural gas employers in Pennsylvania and West Virginia. Responses do not add to 100 percent because respondents were allowed to mark multiple high-priority occupations.
RAND *RR2199-3.5*

try. Its prevalence among employers' reports reinforces the notion that understanding engineering and technology is of value to the industry.

Interviewees for the two upstream companies we spoke with reported that hiring managers vet applicants in the interview process to ascertain their technical knowledge with specific job-related questions. In one company, for example,

> . . . we might ask them, have they prepared a [specific form] for the state of Pennsylvania? So it would be a very specific technical question. For someone in a lease operator role, it might be, do you understand a plunger lift system in a well versus a pumping unit or just a natural well versus a completed well, just to ascertain their general knowledge of oil and gas terminology.

In the other upstream company, applicants for a service technician job

> are asked to read and interpret electrical wiring diagrams; how motors, compressors, hydraulic systems work (how fluid flow works). [We also look for] how they present themselves because that signals how they could deal with clients.

An interviewee with a midstream company that employs welders noted that although most of their employees are union-trained, they still test them within the shop before they go in the field to guarantee that they understand the technical requirements of laying gas pipelines. Likewise, all other applicants are interviewed beforehand to ensure they have the technical skills to work on the necessary equipment. The interviewee commented, "With the on-site work around hot pipes, you really have to know what you are doing. You are running a bulldozer, digging up a pipeline, running other machines, laying pipe into a facility, working with any big equipment like that." Another midstream company asked applicants to demonstrate their writing ability, given the requirement for workers in their high-priority occupations to "maintain records so they are useful to others, write reports from site visits so others can extract useful information from site visits."

Employers Seek Workers with Critical Thinking, Judgment, Decisionmaking, and Complex Problem–Solving Skills

Figure 3.6 identifies the most-relevant skills that employers seek when hiring for their high-priority occupations. The most in-demand skills are critical thinking (reported by 65 percent of employers); judgment and decisionmaking (reported by 63 percent of employers); and complex problem–solving (reported by 63 percent of employers). This comports with an array of studies over the past decade that find that employers consistently report a need for critical thinking and problem-solving skills in their employees (Cappelli, 2014). This does not necessarily mean that applicants or current employees lack these skills, but rather that they are considered by employers in the industry as essential to the nature of the work.

These cross-cutting in-demand skills (such as critical thinking, judgment, and decisionmaking) are far more prevalent in our survey responses than skills that are directly applicable to work conducted within the oil and natural gas industry (such as equipment maintenance, operation monitoring, operation and control, repair, or technology design). Workers need to be sufficiently agile and versatile to effectively consume, interpret, and manipulate information in the context of their jobs. This suggests that workforce development for the industry needs to incorporate course work, training, and experiences that build the skills in talent, and not only focus on those skills relevant for specific tasks.

Indeed the employers with whom we spoke noted that they are just as interested in higher-order cross-cutting skills as they are in an applicant's technical knowledge. Interviewees used such terms as "communication," "teamwork," or "initiative" to describe these higher-order cross-cutting skills. All interviewees noted the need for clear communication and teamwork skills, as well as having a certain "personality type" that worked well with others under pressure. As one example, an interviewee in a midstream company explained,

> The ability to communicate clearly and work well with others can have life-or-death implications; these are dangerous work environments. . . . We realize the danger of a situation we are working

Figure 3.6
Percentage of Employers Reporting Specific Skills Sought for High-Priority Occupations

SOURCE: Authors' calculations using RAND SHALE Survey of Employers (2016–2017); N = 67.
NOTE: Results are weighted to generalize to all oil and natural gas employers in Pennsylvania and West Virginia. Responses do not add to 100 percent because respondents were allowed to mark multiple high-priority occupations.
RAND *RR2199-3.6*

> in; there are hot tap pipelines with gas in them that are pressurized. You have to control your emotions when you work in those situations; if someone has a reputation for not being able to control themselves, we will not allow those people to work in those types of situations.

An interviewee in an upstream company noted that communication skills and an ability to work well in teams

> . . . is part of the [hiring] decision criteria. Our company's competitive advantage is our effective communication. If you can't communicate effectively, information doesn't always flow as it needs to. We make a concerted approach to giving out information and by doing that with the right people and the right information, we create an engaging a team culture. There is less finger-pointing, everyone has the information that they need to do their job in a timely fashion, and the company is more effective and productive.

Another employer in an upstream company that the interviewee described as "techy, progressive, and more youth-centric than older, established gas companies," emphasized the need for employees who can work well independently and take initiative. The interviewee noted that while the company's hiring department administers an assessment of technical skills to applicants, there is not a test for these cross-cutting skills. Instead, an interviewer will ask the applicant for examples of how that person is a "10 for 1." The interviewee explained,

> We're just continuing to hire relevant skill types and personality types; driven individuals, self-starters. Our goal is to find star performers who don't need to be actively managed. We won't be able to find that everywhere, but we want people who approach work that way and produce more than their peers. We spend time focused on picking the right people and getting rid of people who are not [like that], a '10 for 1' employee, [which is] someone with an ability to get things done, and who can provide exponential productivity returns. A star performer.

An interviewee from a midstream company highlighted the need for employees with problem-solving skills, going so far as to describe the need to communicate with clients as a core component of problem-solving:

> We're looking for people that can solve problems and that have a good rapport with clients—well, because that's part of solving problems. It's hard to solve problems unless you can develop a working relationship with a client and kind of form a partnership with the client to get to the root of the problem. It's a little different from most laboratories, where people send samples, they send numbers. . . . Our primary goal is to answer a more open-ended question that the customer has. So we're looking for problem-solvers of all kinds.

The same employer noted the need for workers with strong writing and communication skills:

> If [the employee] hits a problem, they'll often kind of take off on a tangent, and they don't really communicate very well that they're going to do that or why they're going to do that. They don't communicate with clients when they're going to be late on things. They just don't communicate. . . . They are very good technically and particularly very good, as you might expect, with software and coding and computer skills and so forth, compared to the people of my generation. What they are not good at is communication. They don't communicate worth a damn. They want to text all the time. Sometimes it just makes a lot of sense to pick up the phone and call people and not have 75 texts or emails. They are not very good at communicating internally, and they are not very good at communicating externally. I think that's one of the major weaknesses, and they are awful at writing. They can't write to save their life.

Collectively, these quotes from our in-depth interviews corroborate the findings from the survey that indicate a need by employers for workers with cross-cutting employability skills.

Employers Look to On-the-Job Training to Meet Their Skills Needs

When we asked about the kinds of internal training and development activities that companies use to meet the skills needs for these high-priority occupations, we found that the majority (67 percent) of employers turn to on-the-job training. Mentoring and coaching was also a commonly used model, with 45 percent of respondents selecting that option. Eighteen percent of employers did not provide any internal professional development opportunities for their employees. These results are presented in Figure 3.7.

Figure 3.7
Percentage of Employers Reporting Training Provided to Employees to Meet Skills Needs in High-Priority Occupations

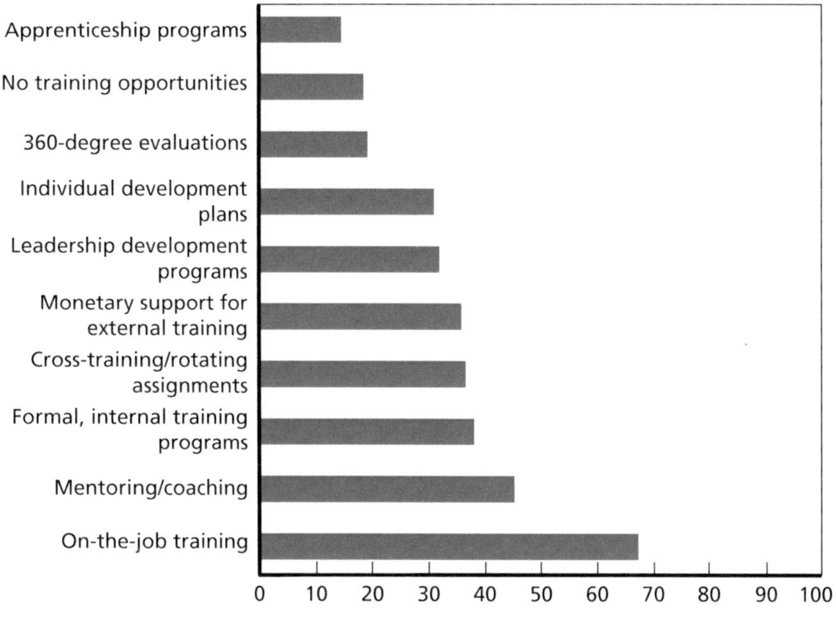

SOURCE: Authors' calculations using RAND SHALE Survey of Employers (2016–2017).
NOTE: N = 67. Results are weighted to generalize to all oil and natural gas employers in Pennsylvania and West Virginia. Responses do not add to 100 percent because respondents were allowed to mark multiple high-priority occupations.
RAND *RR2199-3.7*

Discussion

The analyses summarized in this chapter sought to identify the workforce needs of employers in the oil and gas industry. Whereas past research has largely focused on projections of specific occupations that are expected to grow and contract, our study seeks to understand the contours of this demand from the perspective of employers. Two findings stand out as critical.

First, a sizable number of high-priority occupations require long-term training and require more than five years of work experience to perform the tasks competently. While workforce development policy discussions and resulting policy initiatives tend to focus on the school-to-work transition, our survey findings underscore the need for ongoing training and professional development after hiring to ensure that employees are getting training both for the jobs they currently have *and for the jobs they might take in the future*. Focusing on the workforce as a pipeline that support *careers* rather than a single hiring transaction at entry is essential for sustaining the oil and natural gas industry over the long term. Put differently, the contours of workers' careers will evolve over time, requiring additional training, guidance, support, and (in some cases) additional degrees or certifications. Focusing only on the education, knowledge, and skills that workers gain from school and bring with them to their jobs is potentially short-sighted.

Second, the knowledge and skills most needed by employers are ones that are *cross-cutting*. Employers want workers who can think critically and creatively in the context of their work, solve work-based problems, and make sound decisions at work. They also want workers who understand the fundamentals of administration and management. Few will argue that improving such knowledge and skills is not a worthy policy goal, but we should note there is nothing in our data to suggest who is best to impart these knowledge and skills (i.e., schools, employers, or another entity entirely) or even who should bear the cost of these investments. We contend only that such knowledge and skills are needed by employers and that solutions to improve workforce development should include serious consideration of how workers can best attain them.

Although it is clear from this study's survey results and the comments provided by our interviewees that cross-cutting skills are vital, these skills were rarely mentioned when employers described the content of their on-the-job training programs. This suggests that employers may desire such skills but are not directly cultivating them among current employees. This is problematic; such cross-cutting skills may not necessarily be acquired in a postsecondary STEM degree program, even those in which workplace experiences or internships are embedded. Therefore, employers have sought to identify job applicants with these skills (or the foundations to develop them) as an essential part of the hiring process. Unlike the different forms of knowledge that can be indirectly—albeit imperfectly—traced to educational credentials on a resume (e.g., a bachelor's degree in engineering should convey knowledge in "engineering and technology"), it is less clear how employers evaluate applicants or their current employees with respect to cross-cutting employability skills. If employers need these skills in their workers for high-priority jobs, how do they know who has them and who needs them?

With this basic understanding of the needs of employers in mind, a logical next question is: How well equipped are colleges in the region to meet the needs of employers? Assessing the ability of colleges in the region to support workforce development will help us better understand barriers to and opportunities for meeting the needs of employers in the industry. Chapter Four provides such an assessment.

CHAPTER FOUR

Supplying Credentials, Courses, and Training Opportunities: What Colleges Provide

We now turn our attention to assessing the extent to which colleges in the region report that their institutions provide credentials, courses, and training opportunities that impart the knowledge and skills identified as necessary by employers in the oil and natural gas industry. To accomplish this, we draw on data from our SHALE Survey of Education and Training Providers, which include responses from 87 colleges (both two-year and four-year schools), universities, and trade schools in Ohio, Pennsylvania, and West Virginia. Recall that this survey was filled out by chairs of engineering and science departments at bachelor degree–bearing four-year schools and by chairs of oil and natural gas programs at associate's degree–bearing or certificate and licensure schools. Although not all job seekers will come from these departments and programs, these are the central ones that educate students seeking careers in the oil and natural gas industry. For ease of expression, we collectively refer to our sample simply as "colleges" or "departments" throughout the chapter, but keep in mind these are institutions with programs specific to the oil and natural gas industry.

In this chapter, we make a number of strategic comparisons between responses of employers (from the previous chapter) and those of colleges, looking for concordance or discordance between what employers say they need and what colleges say they provide. However, we urge readers to interpret the findings with caution. Colleges vary substantially in the sizes of their student bodies; similarly, employers vary substantially in the number of workers they hire and employ. Should we find evidence that colleges are addressing skills-gap issues per their responses to the survey, that does not necessarily mean they are producing enough graduates to fulfill labor demands. Moreover, the tristate region is geographically dispersed (covering approximately 115,000 square miles), so training opportunities at colleges may not be feasible for all workers, depending on their location and resources. With these qualifications in mind, we focus our attention on broad patterns where notable differences are observed.

Colleges in the Region Do Not Explicitly Incorporate Cross-Cutting Employability Skills in Their Programming

In the previous chapter, we found that the knowledge and skills that employers needed most for their high-priority occupations were technical, computer, and cross-cutting skills such as time management, speaking, team-building, and writing. RAND's SHALE survey asked department heads at colleges in the region to report if they offered coursework or instruction providing certain knowledge and skills. We inquired about the same content knowledge and skill that we asked of employers. We first show the distribution of content knowledge that colleges reported providing (Figure 4.1). Note that we list the content knowledge in *descending* order based on the extent of demand as reported by employers (Figure 3.5 in Chapter Three), with those toward the top being reported most often by employers as in demand and those toward the bottom reported by employers as in less demand. In other words, looking top to bottom in the figure, the form of knowledge most needed by employers is knowledge of administration and management, whereas the form of knowledge least needed by employers is knowledge of psychology.

If there were a perfect symbiotic relationship between employer needs and local training opportunities in the tristate region's workforce development system, we would expect that the size of the bars would be largest toward the top of the Figure (meaning that a large number of college were explicitly providing instruction on the knowledge most in demand) and smallest toward the bottom of the Figure (meaning that a small number of colleges were explicitly providing instruction on the

Figure 4.1
Percentage of Colleges That Offer Coursework or Instruction on Specific Knowledge That Employers Seek for High-Priority Occupations

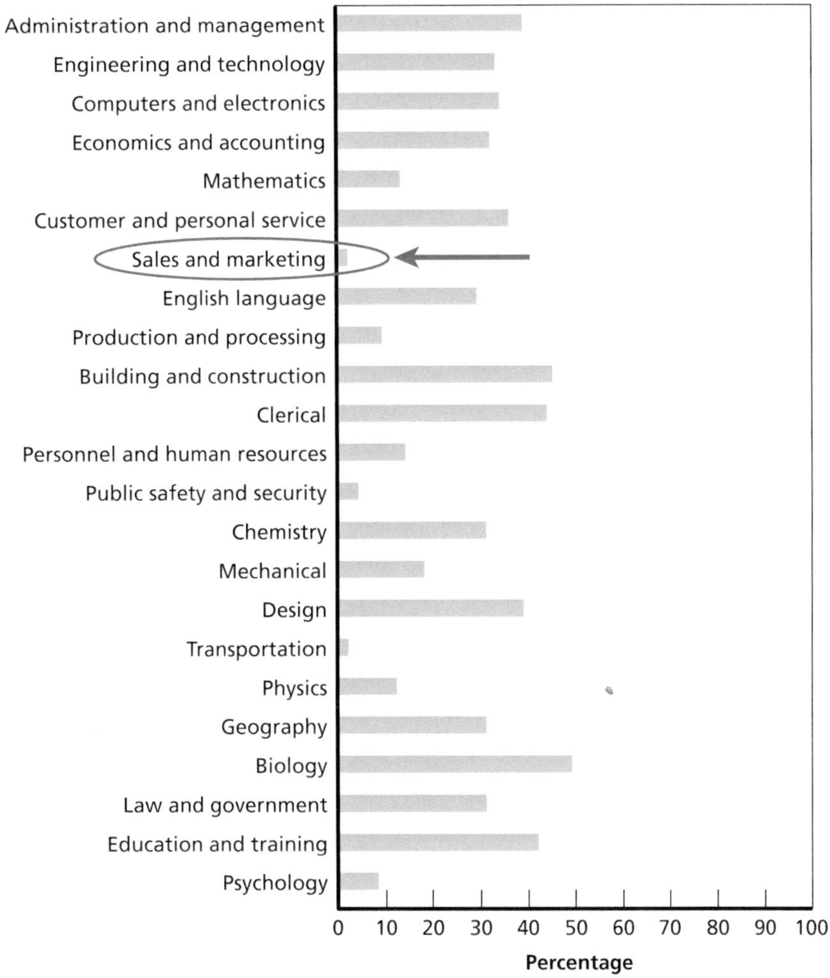

SOURCE: Authors' calculations using RAND SHALE Survey of Education and Training Institutes (2016–2017).
NOTE: N = 87. Results are weighted to generalize to all postsecondary institutions in Ohio, Pennsylvania, and West Virginia. Responses do not add to 100 percent because respondents were allowed to mark multiple forms of knowledge.
RAND *RR2199-4.1*

knowledge least in demand). While we do not see such a pattern, we do see that a sizable number of colleges offer instruction on the forms of knowledge that are in greatest demand. For example, more than one-third of colleges reported offering coursework or instruction in administration and management (39 percent), engineering and technology (33 percent), and computers and electronics (34 percent).

Although there are colleges in the region that include the highest-demand types of content knowledge in their curricula, one notable exception is for sales and marketing content: 28 percent of employers noted they were looking for workers who understood sales and marketing for their employment in their high-priority occupations, but here we see that only 2 percent of colleges reported providing such knowledge as part of their degree programs geared toward the oil and gas industry. This is not altogether surprising, given that sales and marketing are typical components of business degree programs. However, the fact that such knowledge is sought by employers in the industry suggests that business courses might be valuable to incorporate into oil and gas–specific degree programs.

Next, we show the distribution of skills that colleges reported providing (Figure 4.2). As with our presentation of forms of knowledge, we list skills in *descending* order based on the extent of demand as reported by employers (as presented in Figure 3.6 in Chapter Three). Looking top to bottom in the figure, employers are most in need of employees with critical thinking skills and least in need of employees with skills in management of financial resource.

There are two main findings of note here. First, the majority of colleges (66 percent) report that their oil and natural gas–focused departments specifically focus on critical thinking skills. In fact, critical thinking skills are the most prevalent skills across all colleges in our sample. This is notable because this is the skill most in demand by employers (reported by 65 percent) for their high-priority occupations. Issues of the exact definition and practice of critical thinking skills aside, this being the modal skill reported by colleges suggests that, at a minimum, colleges understand the value of this skill for students in their oil and natural gas–related degree programs.

Figure 4.2
Percentage of Colleges That Offer Coursework or Instruction on Specific Skills That Employers Seek for High-Priority Occupations

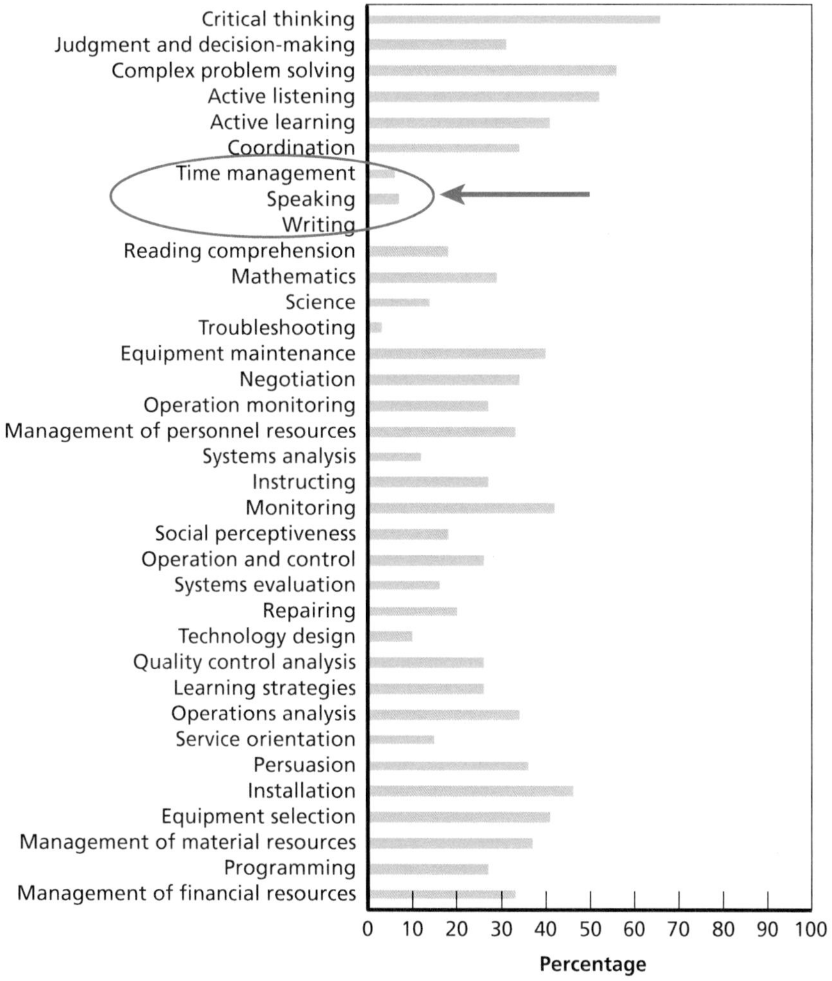

SOURCE: Authors' calculations using RAND SHALE Survey of Education and Training Institutes (2016–2017).
NOTE: N = 87. Results are weighted to generalize to all postsecondary institutions in Ohio, Pennsylvania, and West Virginia. Responses do not add to 100 percent because respondents were allowed to mark multiple skills.
RAND *RR2199-4.2*

Second, time management, speaking, and writing skills—which are in demand among employers—are included far less frequently in coursework offered by departments tailored to students in the oil and natural gas industry. Fifty-one percent of employers sought workers with time-management skills, but only 6 percent of colleges focus on this skill as part of their oil and natural programs. Similarly, 50 percent of employers sought workers with speaking skills and 48 percent of employers sought workers with writing skills, but 0 percent and 7 percent of colleges focused on those skills, respectively, as part of their oil and natural gas programs. The small number of colleges that explicitly incorporate time management, speaking, and writing skills suggests a potential area of improvement in the regional workforce development system. It is worth noting that these are cross-cutting employability skills that are essential for workers in most, if not all, industries—not just the oil and natural gas industry.

Most Colleges Report Supporting Students Getting Jobs in Specific Occupations Within the Oil and Natural Gas Industry but Few Have Stackable Credential Programs

Next, we asked colleges to report whether they offered specific sector-based training opportunities as part of their oil and natural gas–related programs. The option responses in this question aligned with the expectations for career pathways in sector-based training articulated in the Workforce Innovation Opportunity Act of 2014. We show their responses in Figure 4.3.

More than 80 percent of respondents report that their programs are specifically geared to support students obtaining jobs in specific occupations, and 70 percent report that their programs provide content aligned with skills needed in local industries. However, only 28 percent report that they provide stackable credentials.[1] As mentioned earlier, the

[1] It is worth noting that stackable credentials are far more prevalent at two-year colleges. In our sample, 8 percent of four-year colleges and 39 percent of two-year colleges reported providing stackable credentials.

Figure 4.3
Percentage of Colleges That Offer Programming That Aligns with Characteristics of Sector-Based Training

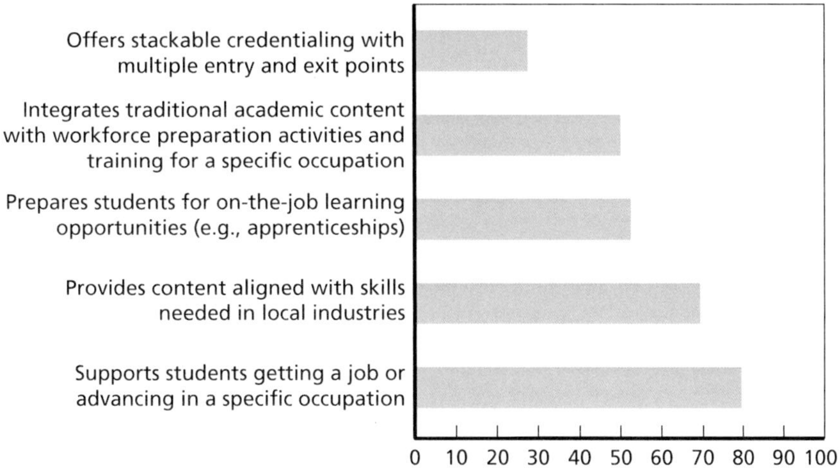

SOURCE: Authors' calculations using RAND SHALE Survey of Education and Training Institutes (2016–2017).
NOTE: N = 87. Results are weighted to generalize to all postsecondary institutions in Ohio, Pennsylvania, and West Virginia. Responses do not add to 100 percent because respondents were allowed to mark multiple sector-based opportunities.
RAND *RR2199-4.3*

U.S. Department of Labor defines *stackable credentials* as those that are "part of a sequence of credentials that can be accumulated over time and move an individual along a career pathway or up a career ladder" (U.S. Department of Labor, 2012). The credentials are stackable in that you can acquire a certification on which you can later "stack" additional credits that count toward another certification or degree. These programs are receiving increasing attention from workforce development policymakers and practitioners because they allow workers to obtain occupation-specific knowledge and skills in an efficient, flexible structure and format. As a relative "newcomer" to the postsecondary credential scene, it is too early to tell if stackable degree programs are more effective than traditional degree programs. Moreover, it is not altogether clear how many schools in a region need to have stackable credential programs for there to be an observable impact on the labor market. The fact that only a limited number of oil and natural gas–related programs in the tristate area offer such programs suggests this might be an opportunity for expansion, should more evidence be brought to bear on these programs' effectiveness in improving the quality of the workforce.

Fewer Than Half the Courses Aimed at Future Workers in the Oil and Natural Gas Industry Use Contextualized Instruction

Last, we asked department heads to estimate the proportion of courses offered to prepare students for high-priority occupations that are taught using contextualized instruction. This form of instruction directly connects basic academic skills to industry-specific knowledge. The hallmark of contextualized instruction is using occupational applications to teach basic academic skills (and vice versa) so that the student learns both simultaneously. An example of contextualized instruction would be using geometric proofs when instructing students on organizing materials for pipelaying in a construction management course, and conversely, using pipelaying examples to teach geometric proofs in a geometry course. As shown in Figure 4.4, the majority of courses offered in oil and natural gas–related departments in the tristate region use contextualized instruction less than half of the time, with 12 percent of courses never using contextualized instruction. Only 10 percent of courses use contextualized instruction all or almost all of the time. We do not have our own data on whether such instructional practices improve knowledge and skill attainment in oil and natural gas–specific programs, but past research shows that contextualized instruction is an effective approach to teaching occupationally focused students (Stone and Lewis, 2012), particularly when it includes "real-world" simulations of workplace situations with actual workplace equipment (Sullivan-Mann, Perron, and Fellner, 2009). In fact, some research indicates that contextualized instruction incorporating such simulations significantly improves critical thinking skills (Abrami et al., 2008; Sullivan-Mann, Perron, and Fellner, 2009)—which, as our analysis in

Figure 4.4
Proportion of Courses Using Contextualized Instruction as Reported by Colleges

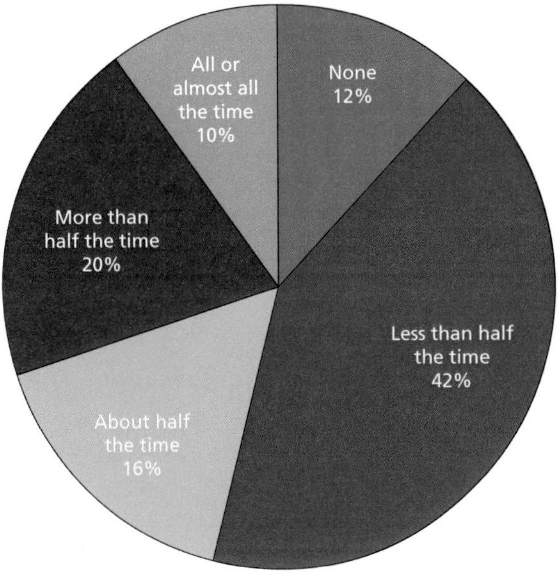

SOURCE: Authors' calculations using RAND SHALE Survey of Education and Training Institutes (2016–2017).
NOTE: N = 87. Results are weighted to generalize to all postsecondary institutions in Ohio, Pennsylvania, and West Virginia.
RAND *RR2199-4.4*

Chapter Two shows, are required by employers for high-priority occupations. Clearly, not all courses can be taught using contextualized instruction. Contextualized instruction is used only "in moderation" throughout the regions' postsecondary programs that feed the oil and natural gas industry—and only about half of colleges report integrating academic content with workforce preparation activities (as shown in Figure 4.3)—suggesting that this is an area for potential improvement.

Discussion

This chapter summarized our findings from the SHALE survey of heads of oil and natural gas–related postsecondary degree programs in the tristate region to understand the extent to which their programs are positioned to meet the needs expressed by employers (presented and discussed in Chapter Two). Other research intended at gauging the supply of workers in the region typically use counts of degree recipients in STEM fields to populate projections of available workers. Though helpful in documenting the broader distribution of educational attainment in the region, our study aims to understand the specific dimensions of these degree programs that may facilitate (or impede) the acquisition of knowledge and skills explicitly reported by employers as needed for their high-priority occupations. There are two major findings of note.

First, most colleges in the region do not explicitly incorporate knowledge of business skills (such as sales and marketing) along with basic skills (such as time management, speaking, and writing) into their oil and natural gas–related degree programs. Though much attention has been paid to occupation-specific skills and the need for these skills among those in the sub-baccalaureate labor market, our findings serve as a reminder that workers in jobs that require more than a high school degree are likely to struggle in their jobs if they have not mastered foundational skills. There is a tension here, in that occupationally specific programs focus on specific job tasks and duties, and thus are efficient in their delivery and designed to meet the needs of students who are often nontraditional (e.g., part-time enrollment, online courses, working while enrolled). With a strict occupational focus and an accelerated timeline to expedite degree completion, these programs are not optimal for addressing basic skill deficiencies in students. Incorporating these skills in a coherent and effective way remains a challenge for schools that desire to better support the workforce.

While overhauling or even restructuring degree programs to improve instructional delivery is often not possible (at least without a lot of resources and instructor training), there is research showing that minor changes to instruction can yield significant benefits. Two approaches in particular—incorporating more writing into course assignments and including more discussion during class time—are relatively inexpensive and easy to implement. Research shows that having students write more to explain their thought processes (e.g., stating assumptions, making inferences, dissecting arguments) and articulating points of view and questioning others points' of view via constructive class discussion significantly improves their critical thinking skills (Tsui, 2002). With respect to writing in particular, recall that *none* of the departments in our sample reported offering courses or instruction that included writing. This highlights a particular area in which these programs can rather easily (and cheaply) contribute to the critical thinking skills of future oil and natural gas workers.

Second, two curricular structures characteristic of successful career pathway sector-based models—stackable credentials and contextualized instruction—are not implemented in the majority of programs or courses in the region and thus seem to be underutilized. As the research base on both approaches is relatively nascent, we are not able to prescribe an exact number of colleges or programs that should offer these curricular structures for effective workforce training to meet the demands of the labor market. Contextualized instruction in particular—especially when it includes occupation-specific scenarios and equipment—improves the development of critical thinking (Abrami et al., 2008; Sullivan-Mann, Perron, and Fellner, 2009). It bears repeating that cross-cutting knowledge and skills are valued by employers, so the challenge remains of how to adopt and adapt these curricular structures (which tend to narrowly promote specific job skills) in ways that impart oil and natural gas–specific forms of knowledge and skill while also sharpening time-management, speaking, and writing skills.

CHAPTER FIVE

Collaborating to Build a Better Workforce

How can the region's workforce development system meet its full potential? This chapter explores the various ways that employers and education providers in our sample partnered or collaborated to align educational programming with workforce needs. We draw on data from both the SHALE Survey of Employers and SHALE Survey of Education and Training Providers. To assist in interpretation, analyses of employer responses use bars shaded in blue and analyses of education and training provider responses use bars shaded in gold. Questions on both surveys asked respondents whether and how they partnered on workforce development activities. We defined *workforce development* for respondents as job training (at schools before workers are hired, immediately upon hiring, and developmental training as workers progress through their careers). We illuminate key findings with selected quotes from RAND's in-depth interviews with purposefully selected employers. Overall, there is not very much collaboration, and, where partnerships exist, they are primarily efforts related to offering on-the-job training opportunities for students in places of employment or are informal.

The Majority of Employers Do Not Communicate Results of Workforce Planning with Colleges

Most institutions of higher education struggle to identify workforce needs in their local communities. In turn, most employers struggle to describe their workforce needs in ways that can be directly translated to competencies and skills that colleges can use to create curriculum or programming (National Academy of Sciences, Medicine, and Engineering, 2016). Therefore, it is critical to document how well oil and gas employers in the tristate region assess their workforce needs and communicate those findings to the education institutions tasked with providing the talent pool to fill those jobs. We inquired on the SHALE employer survey whether and what kinds of workforce planning activities employers undertook with local education providers to meet their skills needs. Results are illustrated in Figure 5.1.

Fifty-nine percent of the employers responded that they do not undertake workforce planning activities with colleges. Thirty percent identify and forward job vacancies to local education providers, and 26 percent provide key information on job needs and future occupational demands: Both of these are the kinds of information that schools

Figure 5.1
Percentage of Employers That Undertake Workforce Planning Activities with Colleges

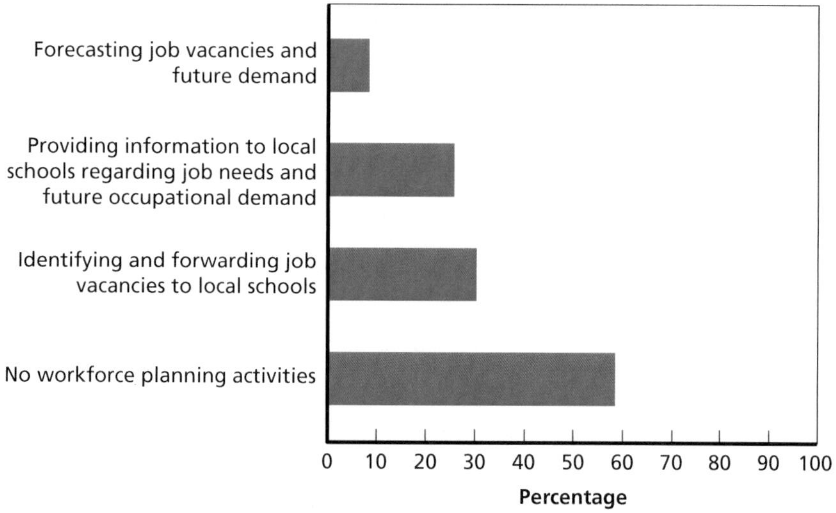

SOURCE: Authors' calculations using RAND SHALE Survey of Employers (2016–2017).
NOTE: N = 67. Results are weighted to generalize to all oil and natural gas employers in Pennsylvania and West Virginia. Responses do not add to 100 percent because respondents were allowed to mark multiple workforce planning activities.
RAND *RR2199-5.1*

need to develop programs and coursework to best meet the needs of employers. Only 8 percent of employers forecast job vacancies and communicate that future demand to schools.

Few Employers Provide Deep or Continual Instructional, Curricular, or Material Support to Colleges

Previous research has demonstrated the value in employers working jointly with colleges to develop curriculum, provide instruction on relevant industry-based courses, offer advice on integrating employability and cross-cutting skills into coursework, or provide materials and equipment for students to engage in hands-on experiential learning (National Academy of Sciences, Medicine, and Engineering, 2016). However, a more typical partnership model is for employers to be asked to be representatives on an advisory board. Board members review programming or occupational standards but stop short of direct curriculum development or other forms of continual engagement (Gonzalez et al., 2015). This more hands-off model was evidenced among our survey respondents; our analyses found that very few employers provided deep or continual support in the form of personnel for instruction or curricular support, nor did they provide material or financial support, as illustrated in Figures 5.2 through 5.4.

Figures 5.2, 5.3, and 5.4 summarize survey results on how colleges and employers partner on curriculum and instruction. Figure 5.2 shows that 64 percent of employers report that they do not offer any instructional support to colleges. The next highest portion of employers (17 percent) report that they recommend or refer qualified instructors to the college. Figure 5.3 shows findings for the same question, but posed to colleges. Here, we see that 56 percent of colleges reported that they do not have partnerships with oil and natural gas employers to support instruction. Twenty-four percent hire recent retirees or current employees as instructors, and 21 percent collaborate on professional development activities. Only 4 percent work with oil and natural gas employers so that the companies' employees can teach at the institution. It is evident from these findings that informal partnerships related

Figure 5.2
Percentage of Employers That Provide Instructional Support to Local Colleges

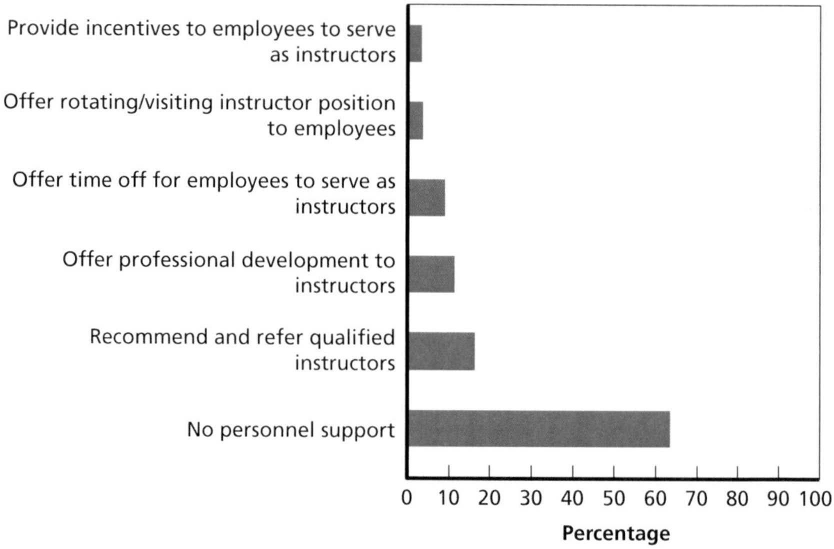

SOURCE: Authors' calculations using RAND SHALE Survey of Employers (2016–2017).
NOTE: N = 67. Results are weighted to generalize to all oil and natural gas employers in Pennsylvania and West Virginia. Responses do not add to 100 percent because respondents were allowed to mark multiple forms of instructional support.
RAND *RR2199-5.2*

to instruction are more typical than formal or structured partnerships. Very few employers in our survey and in our interviews report having formal partnerships. Yet the research literature demonstrates that partnerships that are well structured tend to be most effective (National Academy of Sciences, Medicine, and Engineering, 2016).

Figure 5.4 illustrates the ways that regional colleges partner with employers on curricula development. Forty-four percent report not partnering with employers; almost one-third of college respondents report that employers participate in continual review of curricula to ensure that it comports with job requirements (31 percent) and that employers contribute to curriculum development in *technical* skills (30 percent); and only about one-quarter of colleges note that employers contribute to curriculum development in *soft* skills (26 percent), in

Figure 5.3
Percentage of Colleges That Collaborate with Employers on Instruction

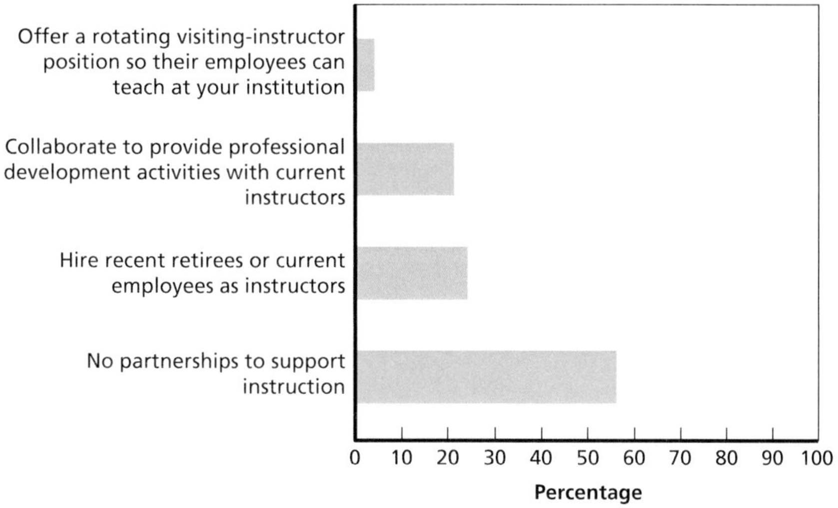

SOURCE: Authors' calculations using RAND SHALE Survey of Education and Training Institutes (2016–2017).
NOTE: N = 87. Results are weighted to generalize to all postsecondary institutions in Ohio, Pennsylvania, and West Virginia. Responses do not add to 100 percent because respondents were allowed to mark multiple forms of collaboration.
RAND *RR2199-5.3*

occupational skills (25 percent), and in development of new curricula based on job requirements (25 percent).

Our findings suggest that few colleges are partnering with employers in the development or modification of curricula to ensure that they are aligned with workforce needs of jobs. Relationships that are already established could be deepened or leveraged to further support a workforce development system across the region, or they could be used as exemplars for other colleges and employers looking for models of collaboration. We do want to remind readers that collaborations are "two-way streets": Our findings here are not intended to indict employers or colleges but rather to point out areas for mutual improvement.

Figure 5.5 illustrates our analysis of whether and which types of educational training materials or fiscal resources employers offer to colleges. Most employers (55 percent) provide nothing. Of those

Figure 5.4
Percentage of Colleges That Collaborate with Employers on Curricula Development

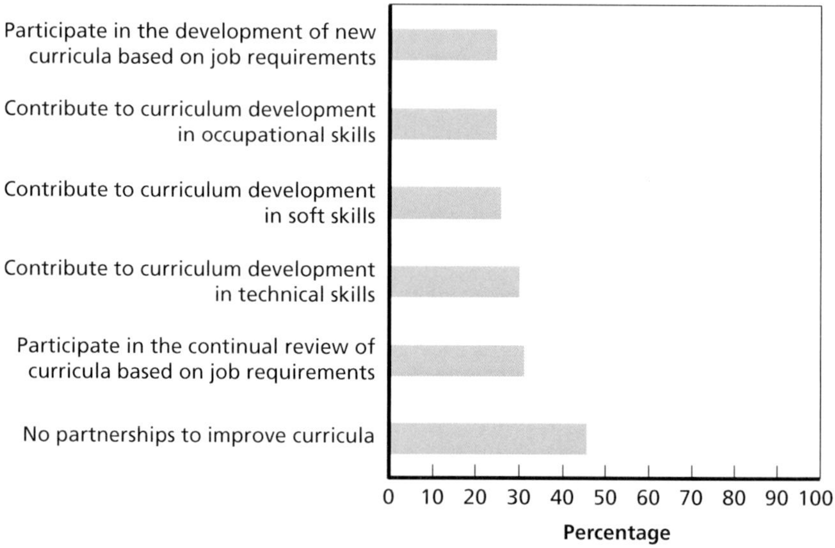

SOURCE: Authors' calculations using RAND SHALE Survey of Education and Training Institutes (2016–2017).
NOTE: N = 87. Results are weighted to generalize to all postsecondary institutions in Ohio, Pennsylvania, and West Virginia. Responses do not add to 100 percent because respondents were allowed to mark multiple forms of collaboration.
RAND *RR2199-5.4*

that do provide support, resources varied: 17 percent of employers offer scholarships and another 17 percent provide supplies and materials for hands-on training. Very few employers provided any of the other options, such as cash-support for low-income students; equipment for realistic, high-fidelity training; or laboratory centers to share space and equipment.

Interviews with employers yielded responses that mirrored the survey results. With the exception of one, none of the interviewees collaborated with colleges on instruction, curriculum, or by offering materials or equipment to colleges and schools. For the one employer who did collaborate, the interviewee himself would guest lecture when requested at the local four-year agricultural college because he had a

Figure 5.5
Percentage of Employers that Provide Material and Financial Support to Colleges

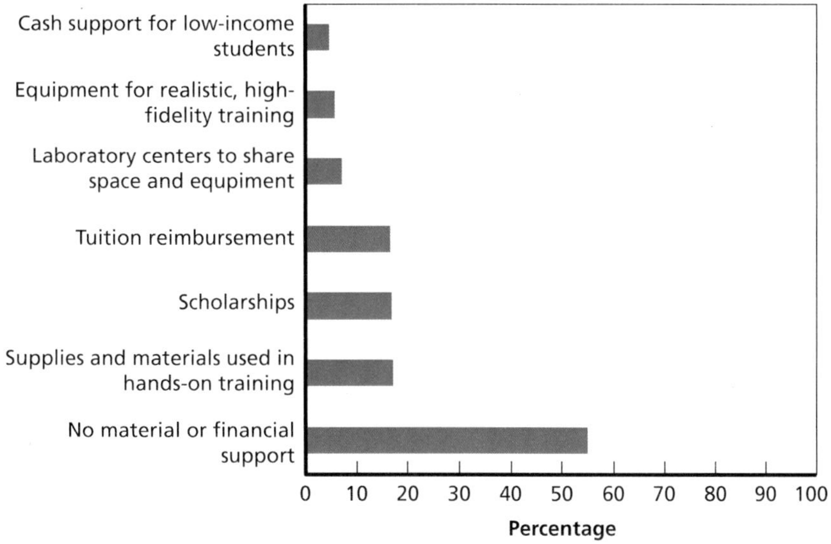

SOURCE: Authors' calculations using RAND SHALE Survey of Employers (2016–2017).
NOTE: N = 67. Results are weighted to generalize to all oil and natural gas employers in Pennsylvania and West Virginia. Responses do not add to 100 percent because respondents were allowed to mark multiple forms of support.
RAND *RR2199-5.5*

personal connection with the professor. These findings suggest that there is limited engagement between colleges and employers in the tristate region on instruction and curriculum, and what engagement does exist appears to be informal and based on a personal connection.

Both Colleges and Employers Point to Unwillingness as the Source for Lack of Partnerships or Collaboration

Figures 5.2 through 5.5 paint a less-than-favorable picture regarding existing workforce development practices in the region: Most colleges and employers do not collaborate or partner with each other. The SHALE surveys inquired about the *barriers* to partnerships. It is important to distinguish between structural hindrances (such as location or lack of processes or regulations in place to allow for partnerships or geographic distance) and attitudinal hindrances (such as a lack of motivation or understanding of how to partner). Figures 5.6 and 5.7 illustrate the responses to the question about barriers from the employer and college perspectives. The survey asked whether the company or education institution experienced any of the listed barriers to having a strong partnership.

Figures 5.6 and 5.7 illustrate that there are varied reasons for the lack of collaboration: There is no single reason that the majority of schools or employers point to. However, the reason that receives the most responses from both colleges and employers is the lack of active outreach from the other. Twenty-two percent of employers report that a key barrier is the lack of outreach from education and training pro-

Figure 5.6
Percentage of Employers That Report Barriers in Partnering with Colleges

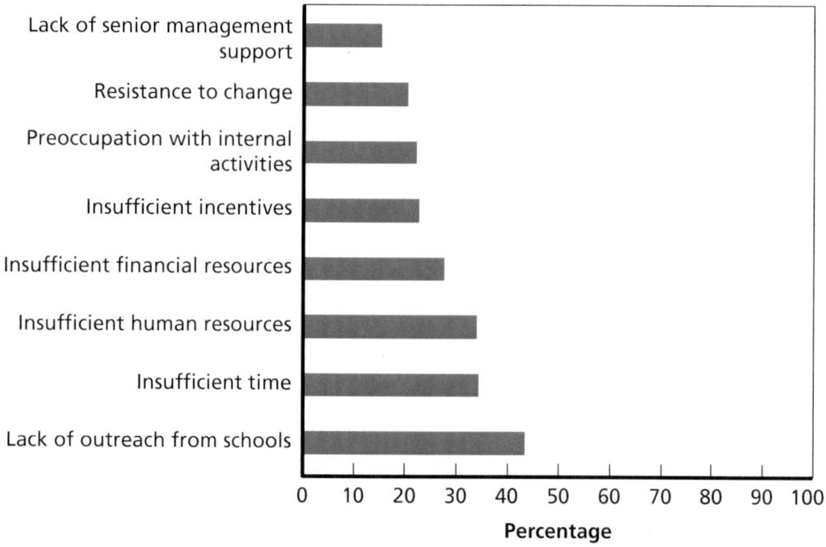

SOURCE: Authors' calculations using RAND SHALE Survey of Employers (2016–2017).
NOTE: N = 67. Results are weighted to generalize to all oil and natural gas employers in Pennsylvania and West Virginia. Responses do not add to 100 percent because respondents were allowed to mark multiple barriers.
RAND *RR2199-5.6*

Figure 5.7
Percentage of Colleges That Report Barriers in Partnering with Employers

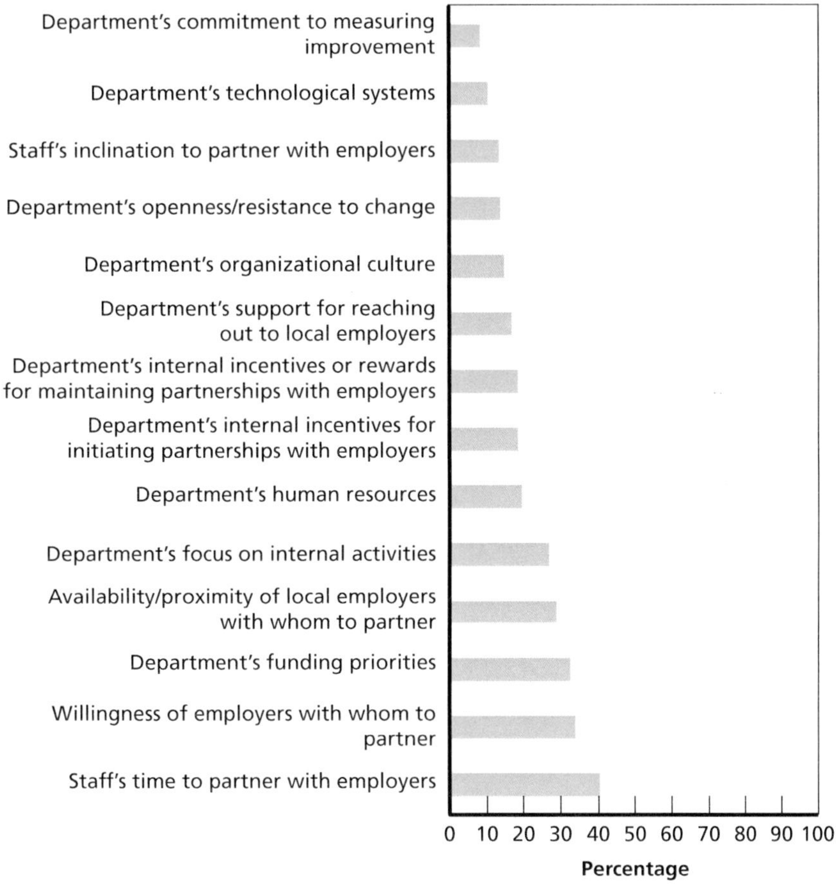

SOURCE: Authors' calculations using RAND SHALE Survey of Education and Training Institutes (2016–2017).
NOTE: N = 87. Results are weighted to generalize to all postsecondary institutions in Ohio, Pennsylvania, and West Virginia.
RAND *RR2199-5.7*

viders. Thirty-four percent of college respondents report that unwillingness of employers is a key barrier. However, the barrier that received the most responses from college respondents (40 percent) was the lack of staff time to partner with employers. Thus, while one-third of college respondents see the lack of willingness of employers as standing in their way, a major issue is time.

Employer interviewees were more optimistic than the survey results indicate. While they lamented the lack of existing partnerships, interviewees wanted to build stronger collaborations and clearly saw the need for and power of such efforts.

One interviewee from a midstream company noted:

> I think there's a great opportunity out there as things will be getting busier in the near future. It's price dependent, obviously, but the programs that are out there—from what I have seen—provide very qualified applicants. I think a better collaboration with the companies, and maybe it's occurring at a level I don't realize, but I think that that is something that can be improved upon and would be beneficial to both those technical programs and the people going to them, as well as the companies. I think it would be a great relationship.

As another example, an interviewee from a downstream company remarked on the need for a sustainable, long-term effort in the region:

> [This company] needs to continue to maintain a workforce in this area; it is not sustainable in the long term to continue bringing in folks from outside this area. The universities are becoming more advanced in this area. For example, University of Pittsburgh is making concerted effort for the engineering school to be more equipped to be able to produce welders and pipeline operators, people on the midstream side. People don't realize that the oil and gas industry is here to stay for a long time, so we need to be able to sustain our workforce for the next 30 to 40 years.

Discussion

As discussed in Chapters Three and Four, while employers in the oil and gas industry have specific expectations and needs of workers' knowledge and cross-cutting skills in their in-demand high-priority occupations, colleges do not offer these specific knowledge and skill sets in their oil and gas courses. Nor are colleges offering courses that incorporate contextualized learning models or stackable credentialing, which could afford more flexibility for workers to move in and out of their studies and work. Given this possible disconnect between employers' expectations and colleges' programming, this study then explored the extent to which colleges and employers are engaging with each other or collaborating to overcome these disconnects. Overall, we find that collaboration is rare, and in the cases where partnerships do exist, they are primarily efforts related to offering on-the-job training opportunities for students in places of employment or are informal in nature. Moreover, both employers and education institutions report that key barriers to collaboration are the others' lack of willingness or active outreach.

One particularly notable finding is that colleges and employers are each relying on the other to initiate outreach to activate collaboration. Further, they report that time constraints impinge on their ability to collaborate. This suggests that other external stakeholders—namely, workforce investment boards and state oil and natural gas associations—could be useful in helping to expedite and maintain these partnerships. Although our study focuses exclusively on employers and education and training providers, these other stakeholders are critical actors in the broader workforce development system. Connecting employers with colleges is one area where stakeholder relationships and resources could bring real value.

Given the real short-term needs of employers in the tristate region, as well as a recognition from our employer interviewees that the oil and gas industry is "here to stay," this lack of an institutionalized sector-based collaboration is concerning. There is suggestive evidence that sector-based public-private models can be successful in meeting the workforce demands of employers and in improving participants' employment and wages: A qualitative analysis found that sector-based programs were able to achieve their stated goals (Pindus et al., 2004), and a pre-post evaluation of six sector-based programs found gains in participants' hourly wages 24 months after completion of five of the programs (Grote and Roder, 2005). Other studies, including a random-control trial, summarized by National Network of Sector Partners (2010), have demonstrated a number of sector-based programs' potential effectiveness. Evidently, a long-term, sector-based strategy to develop a sustainable oil and gas industry workforce is needed.

CHAPTER SIX

Conclusion and Recommendations

Summary of Findings

In this report, we sought to identify the knowledge and skills required of employees as articulated by oil and natural gas employers in Ohio, Pennsylvania, and West Virginia for their high-priority occupations. We also sought to assess the extent to which colleges and postsecondary training institutes in the region support the needs of employers and how companies and education institutions collaborate or partner to link workforce development and education with the demands of this sector. To accomplish this, we analyzed data from three sources: a survey of 67 oil and natural gas employers in the tristate region, in-depth interviews with a purposive sample of six oil and natural gas employers to augment survey responses, and a survey of 87 heads of postsecondary education departments that offer majors related to the oil and natural gas industry.

Our analysis identifies three issues that employers, educators, policymakers, and the broader stakeholder community invested in regional economic development need to be aware of.

- First, basic cross-cutting skills—such as time management, speaking, and writing—and knowledge of business operations (including sales and marketing) are reported by employers as essential for their workers to competently perform in high-priority occupations. However, these basic cross-cutting skills tend not to be emphasized in local postsecondary degree programs that support the oil and natural gas industry. This phenomenon is well documented in other parts of the United States for STEM programs: There is a growing need for graduates with skills outside a core discipline or that are not occupation-specific, such as problem solving, critical thinking, teamwork and collaboration, communication, and creativity; yet significant numbers of students are graduating with certificates or degrees who lack these employability or cross-cutting skills to succeed (National Academy of Sciences, Engineering, and Medicine, 2016).

- Second, a sizable number of high-priority occupations require bachelor's degrees, long-term training, and more than five years of work experience to perform the tasks competently, suggesting that focusing on the workforce as a pipeline that support *careers* rather than as a single hiring transaction at entry is essential for sustaining the oil and natural gas industry over the long term.
- Third, there is a clear lack of collaboration and partnerships between oil and gas companies and education providers across the region: The majority of employers do not involve colleges in workforce planning, and while most colleges rely on representatives from companies to serve on advisory boards or have work-based learning opportunities for their students, very few employers provide deep or continual support in the form of personnel for instruction or curricular support or in the form of material or financial support in classrooms. Finally, colleges and employers each point to the other's unwillingness as the source for lack of partnerships or collaboration.

Limitations

At the outset of this report, we noted three analytic limitations to keep in mind when interpreting our findings:

1. We are unable to directly quantify supply-demand dynamics as they pertain to the number of job openings that require certain skills and the number of individuals available to fill those job openings.

2. Our survey of employers includes only those in Pennsylvania and West Virginia, with none in Ohio.
3. Response rates to our surveys—9 percent for our survey of employers and 21 percent for our survey of education and training providers—were not as high as we had hoped.

Though we feel our findings are relevant and comport with those from similar studies, these limitations place boundaries on what they can tell us about the tristate region's oil and natural gas industry and schools that support the industry.

We would like to raise two additional limitations that provide context for our recommendations. First, though the heart of the oil and natural gas industry in the region is centered around eastern Ohio, western Pennsylvania, and northern West Virginia, our analysis spans employers and schools across all parts of the three states—some outside the immediate Marcellus and Utica shale regions. In covering a broad geography, we recognize that distance may prove a formidable barrier to training and job opportunities. We do not quantify the distance between firms and schools. Moreover, we do not quantify the distance between communities with a large number of job seekers and these training and job opportunities. Should policymakers and other stakeholders actively seek to implement our recommendations, they should take geographic access issues into consideration to maximize the reach of new workforce development strategies.

Second, the workforce development system includes an array of actors beyond postsecondary institutions and employers, such as high schools and elementary schools, government agencies (including local departments of labor and chambers of commerce), workforce investment boards, industry associations, and regional development planners. In focusing only on employers and colleges, the voices and perspectives of these actors are not included here. Our recommendations are derived largely from the findings from our analysis, but policymakers should consider how to make use of the resources and relationships of all parts of the broader workforce development system to ensure that any new directions have their full backing.

Recommendations

The three issues just summarized afford a unique opportunity for the region's stakeholders to improve partnerships and collaborations to strengthen the oil and natural gas sector's workforce development system. A robust and effective workforce development system requires proactive steps by college leaders, local employers, and intermediary organizations or government entities to build and sustain concrete alliances (National Academy of Sciences, Engineering, and Medicine, 2016). Here, we offer recommendations for colleges to be more responsive to the knowledge and skills demands of high-priority occupations, employers to be more flexible in the workforce that they hire and more proactive in engaging with local colleges, and policies that state and local governments can enact to foster a collaborative workforce development ecosystem.

Colleges need to adjust programming so that it fits better with the agile, flexible, and nonlinear nature of workforce development. Full-time, long-term employment with a single employer is no longer the modal experience in the United States. Throughout their lives, American workers have stints with multiple employers, interspersed with periods of unemployment and job searching. Some workers return to school to sharpen their skills, and some change career fields altogether. Additionally, new models of employment are developing and expanding—such as project-based employment, wherein workers piece together multiple part-time jobs, and "microentrepreneurship." The volatile nature of the oil and gas industry resulting from fluctuations in supply and demand makes employees particularly susceptible to shifts in employment (Gonzalez et al., 2017). However, our analyses revealed that the oil and gas workforce development system in in the tristate region does not appear to support contemporary workers with dynamic and versatile careers. Instead, the majority of oil and gas programs in colleges we surveyed were nonrecursive and linear, indicating that education is assumed to be a "one-time" experience that temporally precedes an adult career in a single occupation that builds on the skills and training acquired during youth. This outdated model of programming worked well when a talent pool remained in a single career in which they maintained an upward occupational trajectory with the same employer and/or industry. In our study, very few local colleges incorporate contextualized learning or stackable credentialing, which aligns better with the current dynamic nature of work. Including contextual-learning and stackable credentialing better fits the nature of employment in an evolving, technologically innovative sector.

We want to caution, though, that while flexible strategies for supporting the dynamic nature of workers' careers (such as stackable credentials) are likely effective in imparting job-specific knowledge and skills, they are not geared toward providing basic, cross-cutting employability skills. There is an underlying tension between meeting the immediate needs of employers with specific skill requirements and meeting the needs of the broader system. The former can often be solved with flexible strategies, but the latter is more difficult and often requires systematic institutional change (e.g., STEM degree programs expanding to incorporate employability skills, employers seriously investing in upskilling their current workers). That said, these need not be viewed as dueling priorities: Focusing on one at the expense of other will not promote balance in the broader workforce development ecosystem.

Colleges should prioritize the development of work-based learning opportunities for students, such as internships or cooperatives, that provide hands-on, experiential learning at a worksite. This will require actively reaching out to employers. Interviews with employers across the region revealed that they are eager to work with colleges to offer work-based learning opportunities; they simply do not know whom to contact or how best to organize an agreement. Thus, college presidents or department heads will need to actively reach out to local employers to set up, standardize, and implement a sustainable and practical internship or other work-based learning program that is integrated within coursework. Incorporating work-based learning opportunities within coursework could have the added benefit of exposing students to a variety of jobs, which should improve career decisionmaking, and afford students vital on-the-job experience that our analyses indicate employers are looking for.

Though colleges are vital sources of talent, employers should consider training opportunities for an array of workers, including those coming from other industries and those within their own staff. Our analyses revealed that the high-priority occupations in most demand required a minimum of five years of experience, yet employers reported that they had difficulty finding the right types of workers to fill these jobs. Employers, therefore, have three options to ensure that high-priority occupations are filled: Look for nontraditional applicants who have moved across jobs and industries and have the years of experience but could be "trained up" in a particular occupation; upskill and develop their incumbent workers; or offer opportunities for entry-level applicants to gain the knowledge and cross-cutting skills while on the job. None of these options are short-term fixes; they will require long-term planning.

Partnerships to institutionalize workforce development and planning should include a variety of higher education institutions and other stakeholders. Though much attention has been paid to the development of sub-baccalaureate programs that provide certificates, occupational licenses, and associate's degrees that are clearly in need for middle-skill jobs, four-year colleges and universities should remain part of the conversation. Our analysis finds that despite the acute demand for very specific technical needs of occupations, the lion's share of employers (88 percent) report high-priority occupations that require a bachelor's degree. As a broader workforce development system, we need to be mindful of the array of occupations required to sustain a thriving regional oil and natural gas economy, and not just those for unskilled entry-level employees. Four-year colleges and universities typically have greater capacity for research and development than do community colleges and training institutes, and accordingly can serve as effective partners with industry to expand the pool of workers with top-notch STEM training. Additionally, other stakeholders—such as workforce investment boards and industry trade associations—can help serve to initiate and sustain such partnerships.

APPENDIX

Employer Interview Protocol

Introduction

We'd first like to understand a bit about your organization and your role here.

1. What's your position at this company? What are your roles and responsibilities in that position? How long have you been in your current position?
2. Could you share some information about the workforce at your company?
   a. Number of employees?
   b. Employed in what kind of jobs/occupations?
   c. Where located geographically?

Fulfilling Workforce Needs

3. What are the high-demand occupations that your company is looking for?
4. What knowledge, skills, and abilities (KSAs) do you expect new hires in your company to have?

PROBE:

   a. *Content knowledge (e.g., "math")*
   b. *Performance skills (e.g., "they should be good with their hands")*
   c. *Abilities (e.g., "critical thinking")*
   d. *Workplace competencies/soft skills (e.g., "showing up on time," "demonstrate they can hold a job")*

PROBE:

Ask respondent to "unpack" each KSA. For example, ask "Can you give me some specific examples by what you mean by [_________] Or, "What do you mean by [______________]? Which jobs require what kinds of knowledge, skill, or ability?"

5. In what ways does your company determine if an applicant or new employee has those KSAs?
   a. Are there any specific types of credentials or licensing your company seeks in new employees?
   b. Does your company have job descriptions that list these requirements?
   c. Do you require applicants to take any types of tests (e.g., drug or ability test)?
   d. Any kinds of questions you ask in the interview?

6. What internal processes, if any, does your company go through in order to determine what KSAs a specific job requires?

PROBE: What role do HR/hiring managers, department managers, or other employees have in determining the required skills? How about government regulations (e.g., OSHA requirements for safety certifications)?

7. How well do you think current education or training providers are skilling up the talent in these occupations or skills?
   a. Do you have any concerns regarding students mastering the skills that are being taught? In what ways?
8. Are you having success in finding people to fill your high-demand occupations or with those key skills?
   a. If YES: How are you doing that? What are your tactics?
   a. If NO: Why not? What do you think needs to happen in order for your company to be able to fill those jobs?

On-the-Job Training

9. What kind of on-the-job training opportunities does your company offer? *(Obtain details on how programs are structured, who is targeted population [new hires, incumbent workers, students, etc.], length/duration, and goals.)*
   a. Student internships (before someone is hired)
   b. Partnerships with any education providers
   c. Apprenticeships (being paid while trained up)

d. New hire/incumbent worker skilling
e. Paid schooling opportunities (e.g., tuition reimbursements)
f. Other

Company's Engagement with Education and Training Providers

I'd like to now find out more about your company/organization's work with education and training providers. First, does your company collaborate, partner, or interact with any local education providers?
(IF NO, then go to Q14). IF YES, ASK Q10 through Q13:

10. Which local education and training providers does your company typically interact with?
11. In what ways does your company interact or engage with them *(list out all the ways with all the institutions. For example: curriculum development, your employees guest lecturing in a class, internships, offering students tours of your facilities, sharing data on workforce needs with the school, interviewing their graduates)?*
12. What does the collaboration process look like (i.e., meetings, student-employer interactions, planning and implementation of programs, etc.)?
13. To date, what are some positive and negative experiences your company has had?

Wrap Up

14. In an ideal world, how would employers and education/training providers collaborate to ensure that your company gets the right type of employees?

References

Abrami, Philip C., Robert M. Bernard, Evgueni Borokhovski, Anne Wade, Michael A. Surkes, Rana Tamim, and Dai Zhang, "Instructional Interventions Affecting Critical Thinking Skills and Dispositions: A Stage 1 Meta-Analysis," *Review of Educational Research*, Vol. 78, No. 4, 2008, pp. 1102–1134.

"Appalachia Partnership Initiative," web page, RAND Corporation, undated. As of September 7, 2017:
https://www.rand.org/education/projects/appalachia-partnership-initiative.html

Baird, Matthew, Robert Bozick, and Mark Harris, *Postsecondary Education and STEM Employment in the United States: An Analysis of National Trends with a Focus on the Oil and Natural Gas Industry*, Santa Monica, Calif.: RAND Corporation, RR-2115-AMPI, forthcoming in late 2017.
https://www.rand.org/pubs/research_reports/RR2115.html

Biden, Joseph, Vice President of the United States, *Ready-to-Work: Job-Driven Training and American Opportunity*, Washington, D.C.: The White House, July 2014.

Burning Glass Technologies, Council for Adult and Experiential Learning, and Allegheny Conference on Community Development, *Inflection Point: Supply, Demand, and the Future of Work in the Pittsburgh Region*, 2016. As of June 30, 2017:
http://www.alleghenyconference.org/wp-content/uploads/2016/08/InflectionPoint.pdf

Cappelli, Peter, *Skill Gaps, Skill Shortages, and Skill Mismatches: Evidence for the United States*, Cambridge, Mass.: National Bureau of Economic Research, 2014.

Career One Stop, website, U.S. Department of Labor, undated. As of September 7, 2017:
https://www.careeronestop.org/jobsearch/plan/research-employers.aspx

Center for Energy Workforce Development, *2014 Goals*, fact sheet, undated. As of June 30, 2017:
http://www.cewd.org/mem_resources/2014-CEWD-Goals.docx

Dunham, Kate, Leela Hebbar, Deanna Khemani, Antoinnae Comeaux, Hannah Diaz, Lea Folsom, and Shelley Kuang, *ShaleNET Round 2, TAACCCT Grant Third-Party Evaluation: Final Report*, Oakland, Calif.: Social Policy Research Associates, 2016.

Gonzalez, Gabriella C., Sean Robson, Andrea Phillips, Gerald Hunter, and David S. Ortiz, *Energy-Sector Workforce Development in West Virginia: Aligning Community College Education and Training with Needed Skills*, Santa Monica, Calif.: RAND Corporation, RR-812-NETL, 2015. As of June 30, 2017: https://www.rand.org/pubs/research_reports/RR812.html

Gonzalez, Gabriella C., Kyle Siler-Evans, Gerald Hunter, and Matthew D. Baird, *Wages, Employment, and STEM Education in Ohio, Pennsylvania, and West Virginia: Report No. 1 (2016)*, Santa Monica, Calif.: RAND Corporation, RR-1357-CHC, 2016. As of June 30, 2017: https://www.rand.org/pubs/research_reports/RR1357.html

Gonzalez, Gabriella C., Kyle Siler-Evans, Gerald Hunter, and Nicholas Broten, *Wages, Employment, and STEM Education in Ohio, Pennsylvania, and West Virginia: Report No. 2 (2017)*, Santa Monica, Calif.: RAND Corporation, RR-1863-CHC, 2017. As of June 30, 2017: https://www.rand.org/pubs/research_reports/RR1863.html

Gonzalez, Gabriella C., Reema Singh, Rita Karam, and David S. Ortiz, *Energy-Sector Workforce Development in Southwestern Pennsylvania: Aligning Education and Training with Innovation and Needed Skills*, Santa Monica, Calif.: RAND Corporation, RR-807-NETL, 2014. As of June 30, 2017: https://www.rand.org/pubs/research_reports/RR807.html

Grote, Mae Watson, and Anne Roder, *Setting the Bar High: Findings from the National Sectoral Employment Initiative*, New York: Public/Private Ventures, 2005.

Harper-Anderson, Elise, "Measuring the Connection Between Workforce Development and Economic Development: Examining the Role of Sectors for Local Outcomes," *Economic Development Quarterly*, Vol. 22, No. 2, May 2008, pp. 119–135.

Hausman, Catherine, and Ryan Kellogg, *Welfare Distributional Impacts of Shale Gas*, Cambridge, Mass.: National Bureau of Economics Research, NBER Working Paper No. 21115, April 2015. As of June 30, 2017: http://www.nber.org/papers/w21115

IHS Global Inc., *Minority and Female Employment in the Oil and Natural Gas and Petrochemical Industries, 2015–2035*, Washington, D.C.: American Petroleum Institute, March 2016.

King, Christopher T., and Heath J. Prince, "Moving Sectoral and Career Pathway Programs from Promise to Scale," in Carl Van Horn, Tammy Edwards, and Todd Greene, eds., *Transforming U.S. Workforce Development Policies for the 21st Century*, Kalamazoo, Mich.: W.E. Upjohn Institute for Employment Research, 2015.

Kochan, Thomas, David Finegold, and Paul Osterman, "Who Can Fix the 'Middle-Skills' Gap?" *Harvard Business Review*, December 2012, pp. 2101–2108

Lendel, Iryna, Andrew R. Thomas, Bryan Townley, Thomas Murphy, and Ken Kalynchuk, *Economics of Utica Shale in Ohio: Workforce Analysis*, Cleveland, Ohio: Urban Publications, September 2015. As of June 30, 2017:
http://engagedscholarship.csuohio.edu/urban_facpub/1330

Lerman, Robert, *Do Employers Train Enough? Theory, Evidence and Implications for Policy*, Washington, D.C.: National Academies of Science, commissioned paper, Study on the Supply Chain for Middle-Skill Jobs, 2015.

Marcellus Shale Coalition, "Pennsylvania's Impact Fee: Benefiting Communities All Across the Commonwealth," fact sheet, 2016. As of June 30, 2017:
http://marcelluscoalition.org/wp-content/uploads/2016/08/Impact-Fee-Fact-Sheet.pdf

Moretti, Enrico, *The New Geography of Jobs*, Boston, Mass.: Mariner Books, Houghton Mifflin, 2013.

National Academy of Sciences, Engineering, and Medicine, *Promising Practices for Strengthening the Regional STEM Workforce Development Ecosystem*, Washington, D.C.: National Academies Press, 2016.

National Center for Education Statistics, search page, undated. As of September 7, 2017:
https://nces.ed.gov/collegenavigator/

National Network of Sector Partners, *From Hidden Costs to High Returns: Unlocking the Potential of the Lower-Wage Workforce*, Oakland, Calif.: Center for Community Economic Development, Insight Center for Community Economic Development, 2010.

National Research Council, *Emerging Workforce Trends in the U.S. Energy and Mining Industries: A Call to Action*, Washington, D.C.: National Academies Press, 2013. As of June 30, 2017:
http://www.nap.edu/catalog.php?record_id=18250

National Science Foundation, "STEM Education Data," web page, 2011. As of June 30, 2017:
https://nsf.gov/nsb/sei/edTool/data/college-15.html

National Science and Technology Council, *Federal Science, Technology, Engineering, and Mathematics (STEM) Education 5-Year Strategic Plan: A Report from the Committee on STEM Education National Science and Technology Council*, Washington, D.C.: The White House, May 2013. As of June 30, 2017:
https://www.whitehouse.gov/sites/whitehouse.gov/files/ostp/Federal_STEM_Strategic_Plan.pdf

Office of the Press Secretary, "President Obama Meets with President's Council on Jobs and Competitiveness at the White House," Washington, D.C., White House, January 17, 2012. As of September 28, 2017:
https://obamawhitehouse.archives.gov/the-press-office/2012/01/17/president-obama-meets-president-s-council-jobs-and-competitiveness-white

O*NET Resource Center, "O*NET Data Collection Overview," web page, undated. As of June 30, 2017:
http://www.onetcenter.org/dataCollection.html

O*NET, "Summary Report for 51-4121.06—Welders, Cutters, and Welder Fitters," web page, 2016. As of September 7, 2017:
https://www.onetonline.org/link/summary/51-4121.06

Osterman, Paul, "Employment and Training Policies: New Directions for Less Skilled Adults," in Harry J. Holzer and Demetra Smith Nightingale, eds., *Reshaping the American Workforce in a Changing Economy*, Washington, D.C.: Urban Institute, 2007, pp. 119–154.

Pennsylvania General Assembly, Oil And Gas (58 Pa.C.S.), Omnibus Amendments, 2012 Act 13, Feb. 14, 2012.

Pindus, Nancy M., Carolyn O'Brien, Maureen Conway, Conaway Haskins, and Ida Rademacher, *Evaluation of the Sectoral Employment Demonstration Program*, report prepared for the U.S. Department of Labor, Employment and Training Administration, Washington, D.C.: Urban Institute and Aspen Institute, 2004.

Pittsburgh Foundation, "Power of 32," website, undated. As of September 7, 2017:
http://powerof32.org

Policy Matters Ohio, "Budget Bite: Severance Tax," web page, April 17, 2017. As of June 30, 2017:
https://www.policymattersohio.org/research-policy/quality-ohio/revenue-budget/budget-bite-severance-tax

President's Council of Advisors on Science and Technology, *Engage to Excel: Producing on Million Additional College Graduates with Degrees in Science, Technology, Engineering, and Mathematics*, Washington, D.C.: Executive Office of the President, 2012.

Public Law 105-220, Workforce Investment Act of 1998, August 7, 1998. As of June 30, 2017:
http://www.gpo.gov/fdsys/pkg/PLAW-105publ220/content-detail.html

Public Law 113-128, Workforce Innovation and Opportunity Act, July 22, 2014. As of June 30, 2017:
http://www.gpo.gov/fdsys/pkg/PLAW-113publ128/content-detail.html

Reeder, Matthew C., and Suzanne Tsacoumis, *O*NET Analyst Occupational Skills Ratings: Analysis Cycle 17 Results*, Raleigh, N.C.: National Center for O*NET Development, 2017a.

———, *O*NET Analyst Occupational Skills Ratings: Analysis Cycle 17 Results*, Raleigh, N.C.: National Center for O*NET Development, 2017b.

Stone, James R. III, and Morgan V. Lewis, *College and Career Ready in the 21st Century: Making High School Matter*, New York: Teachers College Press, 2012.

Sullivan-Mann, Joanne, Carrie Perron, and Angela Fellner, "The Effects of Simulation on Nursing Students' Critical Thinking Scores: A Quantitative Study" *Newborn and Infant Nursing Reviews*, Vol. 9, No. 2, 2009, pp. 111–116.

Tai, Robert H., *An Examination of Research Literature on Project Lead the Way*, Indianapolis: Project Lead the Way, 2012.

Tri-State Shale Coalition, website, undated. As of September 7, 2017: https://www.tristateshalesummit.com

Tsui, Lisa, "Fostering Critical Thinking Through Effective Pedagogy: Evidence from Four Institutional Case Studies," *Journal of Higher Education*, Vol. 73, No. 6, 2002, pp. 740–763.

U.S. Bureau of Labor Statistics, "Employment, Hours, and Earnings from the Current Employment Statistics Survey (National)," web page, U.S. Department of Labor, undated-a. As of June 30, 2017:
https://data.bls.gov/timeseries/CES1021100001?amp%253bdata_tool=XGtable&output_view=data&include_graphs=true

———, "Quarterly Census of Employment and Wages," web page, U.S. Department of Labor, undated-b. As of June 30, 2017:
https://www.bls.gov/cew/#databases

———, "Employment Projections: Employment by Detailed Occupation," website, U.S. Department of Labor, April 18, 2016. As of September 21, 2017:
https://www.bls.gov/emp/ep_table_102.htm

U.S. Bureau of Economic Analysis, "Gross Domestic Product by State," database, May 2017. As of August 17, 2017:
https://www.bea.gov/itable/iTable.cfm?ReqID=70&step=1#reqid=70&step=4&isuri=1&7003=200&7001=1200&7002=1&7090=70

U.S. Census Bureau, "Industry and Occupation: Methodology," web page, undated. As of September 21, 2017:
https://www.census.gov/people/io/methodology/

———, "Educational Attainment: 2011–2015 American Community Survey 5-Year Estimates," web page, 2016. As of June 30, 2017:
https://factfinder.census.gov/faces/tableservices/jsf/pages/productview.xhtml?pid=ACS_15_5YR_S1501&prodType=table

U.S. Department of Labor, *Career Pathways Toolkit. A Guide for System Development*, Washington, D.C., 2012. As of June 30, 2017:
https://www.doleta.gov/usworkforce/pdf/career_pathways_toolkit.pdf

U.S. Energy Information Administration, "Natural Gas Cross Withdrawals and Production," web page, 2016a. As of June 30, 2017:
https://www.eia.gov/dnav/ng/ng_prod_sum_a_EPG0_FPD_mmcf_a.htm

———, "Petroleum & Other Liquids," web page, 2016b. As of June 30, 2017:
https://www.eia.gov/dnav/pet/pet_crd_crpdn_adc_mbbl_a.htm

———, "Annual Energy Outlook 2017: Total Energy Supply, Disposition, and Price Summary," web page, 2017a. As of June 30, 2017:
https://www.eia.gov/outlooks/aeo/data/browser/#/?id=1-AEO2017&region=0-0&cases=ref2017&start=2015&end=2050&f=A&linechart=--ref2017-d120816a.5-1-AEO2017-ref2017-d120816a.31-1-AEO2017-ref2017-d120816a.44-1-AEO2017&ctype=linechart&sourcekey=0

———, *Marcellus Shale Play Geology Review*, Washington, D.C., January 2017b. As of June 30, 2017:
https://www.eia.gov/maps/pdf/MarcellusPlayUpdate_Jan2017.pdf

West Virginia Department of Revenue, "Fiscal Forecast—Fiscal Year 2017," briefing, January 13, 2016. As of June 30, 2017:
http://tax.wv.gov/Documents/Reports/2017/FiscalForecast.2017-2016.01.13.pdf